STUDIES IN FRENCH LITERATURE No. 11

General Editor
W. G. Moore

Fellow and Tutor of St John's College, Oxford

BALZAC:
LE PÈRE GORIOT

by

PETER W. LOCK

Associate Professor of French
University of Minnesota

EDWARD ARNOLD (PUBLISHERS) LTD

41 Maddox Street, London W.1

First published 1967
Reprinted 1971

BOARDS EDITION SBN 07131 5292 3
PAPER EDITION SBN 07131 5517 5

Printed in Great Britain by
Butler & Tanner Ltd, Frome and London

Contents

Note

References are to the Garnier edition of *Le Père Goriot*, edited by P.-G. Castex (Paris, 1961). I refer on occasion to the manuscript of the novel and to Balzac's additions and correction; the Garnier edition gives a thorough selection of these variants. For other novels by Balzac I send the reader to the Pléiade edition of the *Comédie humaine*, 11 vols., Paris, 1959. For material not included in the Pléiade edition the reference (preceded by CHH) is to the edition of the Club de l'honnête homme, 28 vols., Paris. 1963.

It is a pleasant duty to record my thanks to MM. Jean Pommier. Roger Pierrot and P.-G, Castex for enabling me to examine the manuscript of *Le Père Coriot*. I also wish to express my gratitude to Professor Frank Paul Bowman for generous advice and stimulating criticism.

Bibliographical Note

For information on books and articles published on Balzac before 1929 the student should consult *A Balzac Bibliography* by W. H. Royce, University of Chicago Press, 2 vols., 1929 and 1930. Two very useful summaries of more recent Balzac studies have been published by British scholars, the first by Charles Gould (*French Studies*, XII, 1958, pp. 299-323), the second by Anthony Pugh (*Modern Languages*, XLVI, 1965, pp. 91-7). Since 1960 the French publication *L'Année balzacienne* (Garnier) has been giving a valuable résumé of works published and research in progress.

The best general studies on Balzac are by Maurice Bardèche (*Balzac romancier*, 1940, and *Une Lecture de Balzac*, 1964) and by H. J. Hunt (*Balzac's 'Comédie humaine'*, 1959); the latter contains a good bibliography. The Garnier edition of *Le Père Goriot* (edited by P.-G. Castex) gives a list of books and articles dealing with the novel itself. This should be supplemented by Donald Adamson's important article '*Le Père Goriot*: Notes towards a Reassessment' (*Symposium*, XIX, 1965, pp. 101-14) which contains a critical evaluation of recent interpretations of the novel.

6

Introduction

With the publication of *Le Père Goriot* in 1834 Balzac triumphantly asserted his powers as the creator of a complex fictional world. As early as 1829 he had resolved to group several independent works under a collective title (*Scènes de la vie privée*), and he became increasingly absorbed by the problem of integrating his rapidly expanding stock of novels and short stories into a single, unified structure. In *Le Père Goriot* the process of unification was carried decisively forward; it was in this novel that Balzac brought together a number of themes previously treated separately, and undertook for the first time the systematic exploitation of characters whom he had already set in motion in other works. Eventually all the novels published since 1829 were to be drawn together under the heading of the *Comédie humaine* whose thematic unity would be strengthened by the movement of characters from one novel to another. *Le Père Goriot* thus marks an important moment in Balzac's career, and it also provides an excellent vantage point from which to survey the larger pattern of the *Comédie humaine*.

Serialized in the *Revue de Paris* in 1834 and 1835, the novel immediately provoked strong reactions from readers and critics. Balzac, like Dickens, was well aware of the advantages of the serial form, and he played upon the emotions of his readers by exploiting to the full his predilection for mystery and suspense. The public, overwhelmed by the first part of the novel, eagerly awaited the continuation, and Balzac noted that the enthusiasm was greater than for any of his previous works, including *Eugénie Grandet*. The critics, however, acted with greater restraint. Although the descriptive passages of the novel were much admired, the characters were generally considered unrealistic, the action improbable and the moral vision unsound. The figure of Goriot, in particular, was judged extravagant and in bad taste.

Some modern critics continue to find the novel unconvincing and over-written. F. R. Leavis, recalling that George Eliot considered *Le Père Goriot* 'a hateful book', has spoken disparagingly of its 'excited emphasis, top-level assertion and explicit insistence',[1] and Martin Turnell has called it 'one of the worst of Balzac's mature works'.[2] Similarly hostile judgments were made during the nineteenth century, particu-

[1] F. R. Leavis, *The Great Tradition*, London, 1948, p. 29.
[2] Martin Turnell, *The Novel in France*, London, 1950, p. 228.

larly in France; apart from Hugo, Taine and Baudelaire, there were very few generous estimates of Balzac's work. The highest praise came from abroad, from such writers as Dostoevsky (who intensely admired Balzac and translated *Eugénie Grandet*), Robert Browning and Henry James. Individual readers and critics of *Le Père Goriot* will doubtless continue to adopt extreme positions, for Balzac generates a powerful emotional atmosphere and aims at grandiose effects. It is impossible not to take sides—and this is admirable, providing that immediate reactions do not harden into dogmatic assertions based on isolated aspects of the work.

In his essay on Balzac, Henry James refers to *Le Père Goriot* as 'a supreme case of composition, a model of that high virtue that we know as economy of effect, economy of line and touch'.[1] The purpose of this present study is to concentrate on Balzac's method of uniting diverse patterns of experience into an expressive formal design, and to provide a basis for a discussion of the novel as a total achievement. I shall have little to say about the relation of *Le Père Goriot* to Balzac's life and thought or to the times in which he lived. These questions have been explored by other critics, notably by Maurice Bardèche, H. J. Hunt and P.-G. Castex (in his excellent introduction to the Garnier edition). Students will find the Garnier edition particularly helpful in explaining historical references and in elucidating the meaning of popular expressions and slang.

Balzac's rich and vigorous language will at first prove difficult to English and American readers, and the slow movement of the opening pages of the novel may seem to ill-reward patient investigation. Balzac makes heavy demands on all his readers; at times it is as if he is issuing a challenge to our powers of concentration and decipherment. But if we accept the challenge and immerse ourselves in his fictions, we find ourselves involved in a world as colourful and as hypnotic as any in literature. Paul Bourget, recalling his first contact with *Le Père Goriot*, writes that 'l'hallucination de cette lecture avait été si forte que je trébuchais physiquement', and most Balzacians will testify to a similar splendid loss of contact with the real world. The task of the critic and student of literature is to re-connect this fine frenzy with the work itself, and to analyse, if possible without distortion, the forms which have aroused so many violent and conflicting reactions.

[1] Henry James, *The Future of the Novel*, New York, 1956, p. 120.

1. Elements

'Un brave homme'

Some time before the composition of *Le Père Goriot*, Balzac made the following brief entry in his notebook:

> Un brave homme—pension bourgeoise—600 fr. de rente—s'étant dépouillé pour ses filles qui toutes deux ont 50.000 fr. de rente—mourant comme un chien.

From this outline, it is clear that the initial concern was with the figure of the father seen in relation to his daughters. Their respective positions are indicated, in typical Balzacian terms, by precise financial notations; and the curve of the action is already suggested: 'un brave homme—mourant comme un chien'.

Balzac's original summary still serves as a succinct résumé of one aspect of the novel. Goriot occupies a central position in the work which bears his name, and his 'secrètes infortunes' form a major element of action and structure. The description of him as 'un brave homme' is borne out in the opening chapter, and our sympathies are enlisted by the treatment he receives at the hands of his fellow boarders. But neither the original designation nor the image we gradually form of him prepare us for the stature and significance Goriot is finally endowed with. From 'un brave homme' he becomes 'un Père *Eternel*' (97), and 'ce Christ de la Paternité' (238). His misfortunes and sufferings, intensified and dramatized, are given a scope and a resonance for which we are unprepared by such humble beginnings.

This problem of stature is crucial to a critical reading of Balzac. His principal characters are often socially insignificant and morally unexceptional; they do not at once inspire in us that expectancy of grandeur generated by the heroes of classical tragedy. We discover them in provincial towns or behind the counter of a store, surrounded by the objects of ordinary existence. Goriot is a former spaghetti-merchant, gross and ignorant, ugly and shabbily dressed; this man is to become a principal player in an 'obscure, mais effroyable tragédie parisienne' (105). In achieving such a transformation, Balzac accomplished a revolution in the history of the French novel.

'Une pension bourgeoise'

The title of the first chapter of the completed work represents an aspect of the novel which was present in the author's mind from the beginning. Already in his notebook Balzac had shown his intention of setting his tragedy against such a seemingly unpropitious background ('un brave homme—pension bourgeoise'). One of Balzac's most noteworthy characteristics is his habit of approaching his characters by way of their surroundings, and this early co-existence of figure and décor should not surprise the student of the *Comédie humaine*. Nothing, indeed, distinguishes Balzac more clearly from his predecessors than his attitude towards milieu and the emphasis he places on background description. In the long and celebrated elaboration of décor in *Le Père Goriot*, district, street, garden, exterior and interior of the boarding-house are depicted with a minute attention to detail which provides an air of authenticity, actuality—and mystery.

This element of Balzac's art—his fascination with the substance and presence of inanimate forms—has been highly praised by Nathalie Sarraute for whom Balzac's method was revolutionary in that he was concerned with 'une matière dense, toute neuve, qui résistait à l'effort et attisait la passion de la recherche'.[1] It is clear that the opening description is no simple inventory of facts and objects drawn directly from reality, but rather a carefully constructed initiation into the lives of certain persons, a prefiguring of events, and an anticipation of drama. Foreshadowing the appearance of the characters is the place they inhabit, a world which shows their imprint, and which suggests their presence. Clearly there is subterfuge here, since the 'world' described is one invented and controlled by the author; neutral matter has been worked into significant material, re-ordered and re-arranged with purpose and design. The critic's most urgent business is to assess this new reality, to ask questions about the forms which confront him, rather than to test the 'truth' of the fiction against the world it is supposed to represent.

'Membres flasques d'une société gangrenée' (224)

This valedictory malediction by Vautrin aptly summarizes the mass of the boarders in the pension Vauquer. Earlier in the novel Balzac, turning from particular notation to generalized commentary, gives us, on two occasions, an unequivocal image of the sinister chorus which surrounds the principal actors of the drama. Dilapidated clothes and worn faces prefigure brutal and bestial natures (18); the boarders form

[1] Nathalie Sarraute, *L'Ere du soupçon*, Paris, 1956, p. 61.

a petty and distrustful collection of creatures, totally indifferent to the sufferings of others (24). Their animality will finally explode into a cacophony of farmyard noises (202); their insensitiveness will make a mockery of Goriot's death: 'un petit mortorama' (304).

Together they form 'les éléments d'une société complète' (24), which initially appears as a fearsome parody of society as a whole. A petty hierarchy is established (some can afford coffee); they have their jokes, their snobberies, their private language (62). They suffer the despotic rule of Madame Vauquer ('madame la présidente'!) who delights in her personal and economic domination. Balzac's curiosity about this microscopic social unit is unbounded and his treatment of it lengthy. There is fascination and disgust in his portrayal, a careful attention to detail (clothes, mannerisms, speech), and a contemptuous passing of judgment. But he does not penetrate this uncharted territory simply to move and instruct; he skilfully exploits his discovery in the making of his total structure.

'Bien des mystères dans une pension bourgeoise' (47)

A Balzacian novel is composed of a series of surfaces and exteriors which, initially opaque, eventually attain more or less total transparency. Objects and persons must be deciphered and forced to reveal their secrets and disclose their true nature and worth. Characters, author and reader are involved in a journey of discovery and a quest for value.

In an early scene Rastignac, having returned from his first perplexing glimpse of Parisian society, observes, through a keyhole, the suspicious actions of Goriot and witnesses, a moment later, Vautrin's stealthy return (42–7). His curiosity (like the reader's) is aroused by this succession of apparently unconnected mysteries, and throughout the novel he will endeavour to penetrate, piece together and assess these and other fragmentary happenings. The central mystery concerns Goriot. Why is he living in the pension Vauquer, and what is his true relationship with the young women who visit him? Is he 'brave homme', 'honnête vermicellier', 'galantin', or 'vieux libertin'? Why has he become scorned and persecuted by the boarders? What is the significance of Vautrin's remark: 'Hors de sa passion, vous le voyez, c'est une bête brute' (59)? It is only gradually that the reader is able to work his way through a maze of conflicting impressions and arrive at a true assessment of Goriot's character and the private drama in which he is involved.

It is evident that *Le Père Goriot* might well have been placed in the *Scènes de la vie parisienne*, since a major concern is the exploration of some of the elements which make up the pattern of Parisian life. But Balzac finally included the novel under the heading of *Scènes de la vie privée*, emphasizing the particular nature of the drama. The intention here, as so often in the *Comédie humaine*, is to move behind the public events of contemporary history in search of hidden and seemingly unimportant situations which may be as full of mystery, interest and significance as more spectacular happenings; and to express, through the medium of the novel, a drama which, for his predecessors, would have been considered unworthy of serious presentation.

'Bien des mystères' (suite): 'Sphinx en perruque' (115)

The most secretive and elusive figure is that of Vautrin, a cheerful, good-humoured fellow whose quips and japes enliven the dingy pension Vauquer, and who manipulates the marionettes who live there. Outlaw and ex-convict, he seems singularly unfettered in comparison with Madame Vauquer's prisoners. Ubiquitous and omniscient, moving freely in several worlds, he possesses more than one master-key with which to unlock secret doors and disclose skeletons. His penetrating glance unnerves and unmasks, though he himself shows the world an impenetrable and enigmatic exterior. Only occasionally does a violent speech or gesture suggest that there is more to him than meets the eye.

Who is he, where does he come from, what is he doing here? His literary origins are uncertain ('*roman noir*'? Cooper? Byron?). Various 'models' have been proposed (Sanson the executioner, Vidocq the criminal-turned-policeman)—pale shadows of the real Vautrin. His very presence in the novel is a mystery; he does not figure in the original brief summary and he makes his appearance in the manuscript under a disguised name. His actions strike a violent and extravagant note in the context of the petty and pusillanimous society of the boarding-house, and his uncanny power of life and death, together with his fascinating amorality, have proved too strong a mixture for many readers.

Isolated from the total context of the work, Vautrin becomes vulnerable and it is not hard to convict him of crimes against credibility. Further study may well result in a modification of this position; Vautrin-Mephisto, seen as a force in the struggle for Rastignac's soul and as an element in the total pattern of the novel, may prove if not innocent at least worthy of consideration. For the moment it is enough to recognize his presence—and the problems it raises.

'Un véritable océan' (20)

Whereas many of the Romantics recoiled from the reality that confronted them and sought refuge in exoticism, dream and fantasy, Balzac took up the challenge of his age, forcing it to provide the substance and matter of his art. He saw in the France and, above all, in the Paris of his day, a vast and fertile field of exploration. Why set forth on voyages, real and imaginary, through time and space in the search for the stuff of fiction, when what is at hand promises so much 'local colour', richness and variety?

> ... Paris est un véritable océan. Jetez-y la sonde, vous n'en connaîtrez jamais la profondeur. Parcourez-le, décrivez-le! quelque soin que vous mettiez à le parcourir, à le décrire; quelque nombreux et intéressés que soient les explorateurs de cette mer, il s'y rencontrera toujours un lieu vierge, un antre inconnu, des fleurs, des perles, des monstres, quelque chose d'inouï, oublié par les plongeurs littéraires (20).

The search for the strange and the miraculous, the infamous and the sublime, begins with a reality which is close at hand.

Le Père Goriot is, among other things, the discovery and evaluation of this uncharted ocean. The voyage begins in the murky depths of the pension Vauquer to which one descends (7) as if to some silent, sunless inferno. This is the vortex of Balzac's Paris, a region which threatens to engulf those who lack energy and purpose. Above and beyond lies the animated and colourful surface of Parisian society which, viewed from the stagnant world of the provinces and contrasted with the sub-world of the pension, appears as a place of magic and delight. Rastignac is dazzled by its brilliance and returns from his first ball in a state of undiscriminating admiration. But Balzac, while creating Rastignac's dream-world, simultaneously begins to undercut the vision and make distinctions which have escaped his hero. The social wonderland will be revealed as a moral wasteland, where greed, self-interest and vanity are rampant. In itself, this part of the subject is rich in possibilities; and Balzac makes the most of them, filling his canvas with garish colours, discordant tones and brutal contrasts.

'Un homme du monde, un ambitieux' (148)

Rastignac the observer is also a major actor and participant in the private and public dramas which form the substance of Le Père Goriot. His ambitions and 'education' are observed by his creator who, working through his hero and at the same time standing back and judging him, presents an unsentimentalized success story with overtones of the cautionary tale.

Rastignac is a familiar figure in nineteenth-century French fiction—the young provincial undertaking the inevitable assault on the capital. Balzac himself had been engaged in a similar struggle, and he doubtless drew on certain of his own experiences in depicting the adventures of the succession of young men who, throughout the Comédie humaine, leave the stultifying and unproductive atmosphere of the provinces and undertake the arduous pilgrimage to Paris. Many are artists of humble origin, like Lucien Chardon in *Illusions perdues*; Rastignac is a nobleman and his talents are social. He is the man of the world in the making and on the make, a figure not unlike many heroes of modern English fiction, whose anger does not prevent them from coming to favourable terms with affluence.

Balzac's fondness for generalization is evident in his early treatment of Rastignac; just as Goriot is the Father and Vautrin the Outlaw, Eugène is the Student (in the manuscript Balzac began by writing 'L'Etudiant' with a capital e). In this respect *Le Père Goriot* is a *Bildungsroman* with Rastignac's 'education' as a major theme. Many roads are open to him: the virtuous path of self-denial and study (under the aegis of his family), the lonely way of rebellion (under the guidance of Vautrin), the hard climb of social ascendancy (under the protection of Madame de Beauséant). He receives a number of implicit and explicit lessons; knowledge is not denied him, nor is freedom of choice. His imagination and intelligence are perpetually active, and after each major encounter he 'processes' and evaluates the images and impressions received, accumulating evidence until the time of final decision.

His journey, in itself significant, provides the unifying strand in the pattern formed by the other elements in the novel. A temporary inhabitant of the doleful pension Vauquer, Rastignac can observe the antics of those who exist there and is yet free to move into the salon of Madame de Beauséant and, eventually, into Delphine's bed. Drawn into the orbit of the magnetic Vautrin, he contemplates the murky corridors of power open to those who know neither scruple nor restraint. Liberated from this malign influence, he plays Cordelia to Goriot's Lear ('Ah! mon cher enfant, mon seul enfant' [289]) and is the sole witness of the old man's agony. Ubiquitous and perspicacious, author's delegate and reader's guide, he provides a sense of continuity and unity to the particular novel and, eventually, an entrée into the total world of the *Comédie humaine*.

*

A rapid enumeration of the major elements in *Le Père Goriot* suggests a work of ambitious complexity whose scope prefigures that of the *Comédie humaine* itself. Moving outwards from the initial concern with the tribulations of Goriot, Balzac has incorporated into the novel a major portrait of Paris, a study of Vautrin, and a full-scale treatment of the career of Rastignac. The original idea of the exploration of a single destiny has developed into a dramatic rendering of the interplay of a multiplicity of personalities and forces. In rejecting the simple in favour of the complex, in following the fortunes of three major protagonists, and in setting his novel against a contemporary background, Balzac broke with tradition and opened up new perspectives for the French novel.

Our central concern will be to study the manner in which Balzac animates these various elements which compose his subject, and constructs out of them a major work of art. As one re-reads and re-examines *Le Père Goriot*, one becomes aware of the complexity and forcefulness of its composition. Events which may seem at first glance simple and self-explanatory take on a greater density when seen in relation to other aspects of the work; characters, which one tends to isolate and discuss as separate entities, come to be seen as parts of a larger design; themes, viewed together, take on a greater resonance and value. Only when the reader has acquired such experience is he in a position to judge the work. Just as the novelist explores and reveals the mysteries of gestures, words, actions and events, so the reader must attempt to decipher, to comprehend and to assess the total world created.

2. Confrontations

Décor

On entering *Le Père Goriot* the reader is faced with a dozen or so pages of detailed description of the pension and its inhabitants. In order to reach the latter, he must thread his way through a maze of rooms and pathways, and negotiate a mass of furniture and other objects which have cluttered up the place for the past forty years. Unlike Stendhal who confessed himself bored by the task of providing 'le pittoresque', Balzac revelled in the business of establishing settings, and he pokes and rummages his way through the musty boarding-house with ebullient yet purposeful curiosity. His contemporaries had already expressed their impatience (shared by some modern readers) at this revolutionary kind of stocktaking, and Balzac acknowledges their criticism (12)—only to ignore it! And we may well consider him right to do so. Apparently prodigal, he in fact makes a prudent and skilful investment in these opening pages, and it is surely ungenerous and intemperate of the reader to begrudge the twenty minutes required to decipher them.

On the simplest level the establishment of a particular sense of place brings the fictional world into focus and provides an air of authenticity and solidity. The reader, ensconced in his 'moelleux fauteuil' (6), is gradually drawn into a world which, superficially at least, resembles the world he inhabits. Streets and monuments are named, distances calculated, familiar objects encountered. All the senses are involved in the exploration of a reality which is clearly perceived and forcibly made present.

Initially reassured, the reader soon becomes disquieted as he is led implacably, 'de marche en marche', from verifiable district and street downwards and inwards to a building whose particular atmosphere is charged with mystery and menace. Walls, separating and isolating, suggest a prison; furniture and appurtenances evoke ignominious misery and decay. Hope is abandoned as one enters the murk and stillness of the boarding-house whose very sign offers an ambiguous welcome: '*Pension bourgeoise des deux sexes et autres.*' Further exploration results in an increase in tension and expectancy. References to imprisonment are multiplied; the boarders are 'condemned' to live in 'cells'; Madame Vauquer is their 'gaoler'. The presence of death is emphasized ('vieillesse qui meurt', 'Catacombes'); poverty and misery are underscored in every paragraph. A sense of the drab, the decaying and the threadbare prevails ('morne', 'effacé à demi', 'couleur indistincte', 'ternies', 'râpée'). A tonality is estab-

16

lished by an insistence on 'teintes sévères', 'cadre de bronze', 'couleurs brunes', and by the recurrence of the colour yellow—which Balzac frequently uses with pejorative overtones. The description contains no note on cheerfulness ('sonnette criarde') nor promise of fecundity ('fructifications grêles et poudreuses'). Objects are resolutely stripped of their glamour: the statue of Venus, peeling, suggests venereal disease.

Thus Balzac, proceeding by accumulation and repetition shapes and controls his material, organizing disparate elements into significant design. Moreover, he pre-empts the reader's reactions by describing district and pension in terms of effect ('l'homme le plus insouciant s'y attriste', 'horrible à voir', 'triste à voir'); to which he adds his own judgment ('nul quartier de Paris n'est plus horrible', 'plates horreurs'). Never one to disguise his intentions, he points out the appropriateness of his own creation, describing the décor as 'un cadre de bronze, le seul qui convienne à ce récit, auquel on ne saurait trop préparer l'intelligence par des couleurs brunes, par des idées graves'.

Implicitly and explicitly, Balzac exploits his opening description as a preparation for the appearance of characters and the unfolding of the action. Once assimilated, the powerful image remains in our minds throughout the novel, and serves as a perpetual indication of a certain level of existence. In describing Rastignac's visit to Goriot's room later in the novel (148–9), Balzac needs only to repeat a few of the motifs already established ('plâtre jauni', 'mobilier misérable', 'prison') in order to evoke the full degradation of the old man's situation. Rastignac, confronted by this misery, recoils in horror; here, and at other moments in the novel (e.g. pp. 95, 234), he compares his squalid surroundings with the magnificent luxury of the houses he visits. He obscurely recognizes that the boarding-house represents a trap, possibly even a tomb; should he lose his nerve and momentum, he is likely to be condemned to join those whose failure he despises.

Figures

When Balzac, referring to the dining-room in the boarding-house, writes 'la crasse a imprimé ses couches de manière à y dessiner des figures bizarres' (11), it is as if he were speaking of the curious collection of boarders, the majority of whom, half-submerged in their surroundings, seem to be composed of the very substance which imprisons them. In presenting Madame Vauquer, Mademoiselle Michonneau and Poiret, Balzac carries over into the portraits elements of the décor, dehumanizing his characters, depriving them of importance and value.

This process is most clearly in evidence in the portrait of Madame Vauquer (12–14). The filth and shabbiness of her clothes, her cold and

B

pallid features, an air of sinister and calculating pettiness make her an inseparable part of the world of which she is both creator and victim. In the portrait of Mademoiselle Michonneau (18–19) Balzac is less explicit, but by taking up motifs already established ('crasseux', 'squelette'), he succeeds, as he does with Poiret ('espèce de mécanique') in reducing figure to the level of décor. The same is true for the mass of the boarders whom Balzac describes collectively (18); their clothes are dilapidated and colourless, their faces cold, harsh and worn ('des faces froides, dures, effacées comme celles des écus démonétisés'). Existing like 'des huîtres sur un rocher' (39), they and their surroundings form a composite and uniformly repellent substratum.

Against this sombre background Balzac presents his major characters, using terms borrowed from painting to stress relations within the general picture. Victorine and Rastignac form 'un contraste frappant' (20) with the mass of the boarders, Vautrin serves as a 'transition' (22), and Goriot receives 'toute la lumière du tableau' (25). These figures, however, though set apart from the others, are seen in relationship to them: the reader cannot but remain conscious of the general image as he contemplates the particular persons. And Balzac makes implicit distinctions among his four characters according to the extent and nature of their involvement with their surroundings. Victorine is related to the prevailing atmosphere of suffering 'par une tristesse habituelle . . . par un air pauvre et grêle' (20), but she is distinguished by a sense of youthful movement. Rastignac's poverty ('méchante cravate noire, flétrie, mal nouée') indicates a potential kinship with the boarders, but an inborn grace and occasional elegance of dress isolate and redeem. Vautrin's portrait reveals his ability to integrate and even ingratiate himself with his fellow inmates, but suggests at the same time a mysterious aloofness, and a force and energy which make of him a giant among lilliputians. Goriot, the visual focus of the portrait, stands alone. Physically he resembles the other boarders; he is 'hébété, vacillant, blafard' with 'teintes ternes' (38); morally he seems in an even sorrier plight. His decomposing body appears to indicate a vicious existence; the boarders suspect sexual degeneracy or cretinism. In Goriot Balzac gives us a figure who has already been almost physically destroyed and who, cursing his useless body, exists now solely as passion, as heart, as spirit.

Thus the images of the characters are rapidly projected before the reader. There is a strong insistence on the visual aspect, but it would be a mistake to conclude, as some critics have done, that the portraits are 'photographs' with every detail unfailingly included. Nor should one take too seriously the often-mentioned debt to the pseudo-sciences of phrenology and 'physiognomonie'. Balzac certainly read Gall and

Lavater with passionate interest and he does posit a relationship between physical features and character; but the method adopted and the deductions made are part of an intensely personal vision. Balzac establishes a typology (which runs throughout the whole of the *Comédie humaine*) by means of an insistence on certain predominant polar elements—rigidity, mobility; coldness, warmth; passivity, dynamism; opaqueness, transparency, etc. The basic distinctions established depend less on moral or sociological considerations than on Balzac's own theories of energy, passion, and will.[1] Physical traits, selected and organized, are reinforced by a barrage of metaphors and similes; the character is thrust at the reader and at the same time is implicitly evaluated according to his force and momentum. The inert (Poiret) are despicable; the purposeful (Vautrin) are to be admired.

Balzac's general framework permits flexibility and variety. Rastignac is introduced by a few deft strokes of colour (blue, black, white); at this stage he is no more than a potentiality, a personality as yet unmarked by the passions which set their stamp on most of Balzac's figures. Minor characters seem adequately summed up in a paragraph; it is as if they had condemned themselves to such definitive treatment: the portrait is almost in the nature of an epitaph. Goriot, on the other hand, is given in a series of sketches which vividly chronicle his decline; Vautrin gets a couple of pages—and yet remains elusive. These inhabitants of the boarding-house are presented by the author in succession before the beginning of the action; other characters (Anastasie, Delphine, Maxime) come to us later through the eyes of Rastignac and hence are initially idealized and described in general terms. As the novel moves forward these early images are confirmed or modified by subsequent events; the figures, emerging from their frames (or remaining imprisoned within them) are subjected to their destiny and our judgment.

Dance

The arrangement of the figures in the opening pages suggests potential partnerships. After Poiret–Michonneau and Victorine–Rastignac, Balzac momentarily places Victorine between the conflicting 'force' of Vautrin and 'beauté' of Rastignac (24)—itself a significant juxtaposition preparing us for a later confrontation (114). This brief early image is succeeded by an indication of the pairing of Rastignac with Goriot, whose face is considered by the young student to be 'la plus saillante' (25) of those which surround him.

[1] I have developed these distinctions in detail in 'Hoarders and Spendthrifts in *La Comédie humaine*', *Modern Language Review* (January 1966), pp. 29–41.

Balzac seems unwilling to release his figures and set the action un-equivocally in motion. Not that the beginning of the novel is static: the presentation of setting and characters contains a sense of purposeful movement and a progression towards drama. But there are a series of false starts which momentarily disconcert the spectator. The completion of the gallery of portraits (25) would seem to herald a general mobiliza-tion, but instead Balzac moves back to summarize and dramatize the preceding four years of Goriot's life in the pension. A return to the present and the use of the phrase 'époque à laquelle éclata ce drame' (39) promises to reward our patience, but again there is a movement into the past—for information about Rastignac. Thus the eager striding forward towards effects (Balzac is as anxious as the reader) is continually checked by the desire to verify origins and establish causality. And although the action begins its chronological march with Eugène's return from the ball (42), the whole of the first chapter (almost a third of the novel) is concerned largely with revelation of past events and the establishment of perspective. It is not until page 105, in fact, that Balzac declares himself ready to move from 'exposition' into his series of dramas.

In the first chapter Rastignac, moving between boarding-house and society, has discovered connections between seemingly independent figures and groups. Relationships are presented as a series of alliances forming, disintegrating, re-forming: Madame de Beauséant is losing Ajuda, de Marsay is preparing to abandon Delphine, Montriveau is neglecting the duchesse de Langeais, Rastignac himself is rebuffed by Anastasie. Units are fragmenting: Victorine is rejected by her father, Goriot is spurned by his daughters, Rastignac prepares to exploit his family. As the action of the novel progresses all these partnerships and groups do in fact disintegrate; Rastignac alone is able to recover from his rejection by Anastasie by profiting from the rivalry between the two sisters to undertake a precarious union with Delphine. We witness a series of desperate attempts to preserve existing alliances or to form new ones; the characters are engaged in an endless struggle to seek protection against isolation or hostile forces.

Rastignac, constantly engaged in his assault on society, is himself sub-jected to pressures from Goriot and from Vautrin who seek him out in order to exploit him for their own purposes. In the first chapter he has been approached first by Vautrin and then by Goriot, and in the second chapter Vautrin again makes a major move (113–132). Balzac imparts an air of theatricality to this crucial confrontation by means of precise choreography; positions, gestures and movements are scrupu-lously noted. Vautrin, domineering, controlled, deliberate, draws the impatient and mobile student towards him and overwhelms him by force of personality and vigour of language. His loaded words seem to penetrate Rastignac's immature defences and lodging in his mind begin their work of erosion and subversion. Although Rastignac is apparently victorious, he is in reality permanently marked by Vautrin's malign influence even to the point of linguistic contagion: he later finds himself using Vautrin's words to justify his actions and plan his campaign (138).

This scene is typical of what we may call the 'contagious encounter'. Balzac's forceful characters resemble magnetic poles which draw into their zones of influence the impressionable, the impatient and the weak. The interplay of attraction and repulsion (prepared in this case by the theoretical discussion of ideas as projectiles on page 114) is dramatized and stylized by means of movement, positioning and glance. In the next major scene, which follows almost immediately, Rastignac is subjected to the influence of Goriot, and once again Balzac uses analogical reference to prepare the mesmeric encounter (134–5). Henceforth Rastignac finds himself in perpetual oscillation between the 'sublime' Goriot (151, etc.) and the 'demonic' Vautrin (178, etc.) until, having witnessed the capture of the latter and the death of the former, he is finally released and permitted to create his own pattern of existence.

As he progresses towards relative freedom of action, Rastignac frequently pauses to take stock of the existing situation. Each major encounter is followed by meditation and assessment (132, 138, 146–7, 220, etc.). After a successful meeting with Delphine, for example, he is confident that the four sets of alliances he has established represent a successful beginning and an encouraging framework for future operations (147). These monologues enable the reader to recapitulate events and establish a perspective. A similar effect is obtained by means of strategically placed scenes which dramatize existing situations. After Rastignac's successive encounters with Vautrin and Goriot, Balzac gives us a short scene in which the characters enact their thoughts in dumb-show. Goriot, whose animated countenance surprises the boarders, affectionately observes Rastignac who secretively exchanges a glance with Victorine (153); this expressive tableau is observed by Vautrin who, although apparently losing ground, is prepared to bide his time. Another of these summarizing scenes occurs in Chapter III after the murder of young Taillefer (214–16); Balzac sets the troubled Rastignac between the exultant Vautrin and the bitterly reproachful Goriot, and Rastignac is forced into an open declaration of his preference. This technique of symbolic grouping is obviously to be discovered in other novelists, but Balzac gives it a particular forcefulness by his emphasis on the offensive and defensive power of the glance and by his insistence on the magnetic rapports existing between persons.

In establishing connections between his characters Balzac proceeds obliquely as well as directly: individual encounters and suggestive tableaux are accompanied by linking actions which imply association. Rastignac on his way to visit Madame de Restaud becomes splattered with mud; a few moments later Goriot, leaving the house, is almost run over by a carriage (67–9). The full implications of these events will be examined during our discussion of themes; for the moment it is enough to recognize a potential identification. More explicit is the parallelism between Vautrin's self-domination in face of danger (222) and Rastignac's control when faced with the insinuations of Mademoiselle Michonneau (228); here we receive the impression that the latter action is inspired by the former: Rastignac models himself on Vautrin. Analogical actions may become a source of ironical contrast: Vautrin, surrounded and unmasked, is finally revealed in his true colours; some pages later the infamous Mademoiselle Michonneau is similarly exposed: 'Cette figure, qui leur était antipathique depuis si longtemps, fut tout à coup expliquée' (227). Balzac also makes use of the linking action to stress similarity between characters who seem to have nothing in common and who may even never have come into contact with one another. Just as he uses physical description to make unexpected connections among dissimilar persons, so he uses gestures and mannerisms to point up psychological resemblances. Goriot and Madame de Beauséant, for example, share moments of self-absorption which result in mechanical gestures and unconscious utterance, even in temporary inarticulateness. Here, as elsewhere, the reader is brought to make comparisons and identifications which are only hinted at by the author.

Balzac's powers of dramatization culminate in the three major crises of the novel which bring to a temporary or permanent conclusion the lives of Vautrin, Madame de Beauséant and Goriot. The first of these concerns Vautrin, and the scene, referred to as 'drame' (221) and 'spectacle' (222), is presented directly by the author who, refusing to analyse the thoughts of his characters, relies on dialogue, stage-directions and physical description. It is a moment of testing and of revelation: Vautrin, facing defeat and possible death, betrays the instinctive violence of his nature which is controlled by a ferocious effort of the will. Balzac's language, evoking emotion rather than defining it, is colourful and vigorous: he exploits a number of intensifying adjectives ('féroce', 'horrible et majestueux', 'sauvage et logique') and a barrage of images ('feux de l'enfer', 'chat sauvage', 'geste de lion', 'volcan humain', etc.). The melodramatic overtones are in keeping with the moment and the character; the passage is a splendidly brassy crescendo in a chapter written with brio.

Madame de Beauséant's abdication brings together for the last time many of the exotic figures of the novel (278–82). The splendour and animation of the ball momentarily obliterate the image of the abandoned Goriot. But elegant façades thinly disguise a series of dissolutions: Madame de Beauséant is preparing to renounce the world, the duchesse de Langeais has been abandoned by Montriveau, Anastasie is wearing her diamonds for the last time. Even Ajuda, visited by Rastignac, seems in despair over his marriage. Madame de Beauséant, like Vautrin, is faced with a situation which is a test of courage and a revelation of true worth. Like Vautrin, she puts her 'executioners' to shame, dominating the fickle crowd which has come to witness her downfall. Balzac pays tribute to her greatness: if Vautrin attained the stature of 'l'archange déchu qui veut toujours la guerre' (224), Madame de Beauséant is granted 'les proportions des déesses de l'Iliade' (279). At such moments the characters are raised beyond the human and set in a context which reveals their author's view of them and his reactions to his own creation.

The scene of Madame de Beauséant's departure is rapidly depicted; Goriot's dying, on the other hand, is a protracted affair and slows up the tempo of the novel. Balzac, having granted Goriot few moments of articulation, now allows him free rein, and Rastignac is subjected to a torrent of words (reminiscent of Vautrin's great monologue in Chapter II) as the old man, alternating between self-criticism and self-justification, retraces the complex pattern of the dance his daughters have led him. For the first time Goriot stands outside himself and passes judgment. His momentary lucidity increases the pathos of the final moments, and his suffering and confession constitute an atonement; he attains, finally, a tragic dimension. And the religious overtones of his language ('martyr', 'le viatique de votre père', 'expier') help us to comprehend the earlier reference to him as 'ce Christ de la Paternité' (238). Again Balzac brings the character forward and confers upon him momentary grandeur. Soon it will be Rastignac's turn to hold the stage alone; the dances completed, he is left to meditate upon their meaning and to choose his future. Dominating the serpentine form of Paris from the cemetery, he issues his 'grandiose' challenge which is at once a conclusion and a continuation.

*

Stripped of its accessory detail, the action of *Le Père Goriot* is seen as an assembly of powers which, laboriously mobilized, converge, irrupt and destroy. The characters, though they have the semblance of real persons, are best considered as forces, to be discussed in terms of movement and trajectory; the novel is an experiment in the dynamics of

contagion and antagonism. Structurally, there is a marked opposition
between the lengthy introductory section and the quick movement of
the drama which begins to accelerate away as the predominantly
panoramic method of the exposition yields to the narrower focus of
scenic representation. From the beginning of Chapter II the action
takes on an almost uninterrupted forward march and there is an in-
creasing compression of the time sequence down to the last chapter
where the events recorded take place on five successive days. The
multiple strands which make up the fabric of the action are woven
together by means of confrontations, linking actions and summarizing
scenes; there is a strong sense of an order being imposed from above
which results in an atmosphere of tension and strain far removed from
the spontaneous naturalness of a Stendhal. An extensive use of dialogue
increases the theatricality of the novel; it often seems, though, that the
characters even when addressing one another are in reality engaging in
self-expression rather than communication. The overall impression is of
urgency—and solitude.

Balzac works primarily with triangular situations, and the structure
of the novel is composed of interacting blocks of material arranged in
sets of three. After the exposition, the chapters centre on Rastignac
('L'Entrée dans le monde'), Vautrin ('Trompe-la-Mort'), Goriot ('La
Mort du Père'). There are three major confessions and three crises; three
balls chart Rastignac's progress in society. The pattern made up by
Goriot and his daughters is echoed by Taillefer, Frédéric and Victorine;
and Vautrin and Goriot engage in a struggle over Rastignac who is
forced to choose between Victorine and Delphine. Direct confrontations
imply the existence of a third party; the characters have designs which
over-reach the present moment. Each scene carries implications which
go beyond the incidents recorded, and each chapter (including the final
one) ends on an ironically optimistic note. Conclusions are effected only
by means of a violent process of elimination: Frédéric is murdered,
Vautrin captured, Madame de Beauséant forced into exile, Goriot driven
to his death. The characters, linked together by circumstance, ambition
and desire, are united only in defeat. As suffering and fatality, present
from the opening pages, come to claim their victims, the drama takes
on the form of a modern 'danse macabre'.

3. Themes

World: L'argent, c'est la vie. Monnaie fait tout (252)

Specifically, the action of *Le Père Goriot* takes place in the Paris of 1819, and Balzac provides sufficient geographical and sociological information for us to be aware of the physical composition of the city at a certain moment in history. Streets, monuments and theatres are named, and there are references to famous contemporary figures. It is a place of glamour and squalour, of elegant façades and miserable dwellings, a city recovering from Revolution and Empire, its stability shaken, its hierarchies uncertain.

As usual Balzac goes beyond literal representation and fashions his own image of the city which becomes a major force in his work. In 1835 Félix Davin, speaking for Balzac, wrote in the introduction to the *Etudes de mœurs au XIXe siècle*:

> Une capitale était le seul cadre possible pour ces peintures d'une époque climatérique, où les infirmités n'affligent pas moins le cœur que le corps de l'homme. Ici, les sentiments vrais sont des exceptions et sont brisés par le jeu des intérêts, écrasés entre les rouages de ce monde mécanique; la vertu y est calomniée, l'innocence y est vendue, les passions ont fait place à des goûts ruineux, à des vices; tout se subtilise, s'analyse, se vend et s'achète (XI, 225).

This image is confirmed in *Le Père Goriot* by the diagnoses of the major characters and by the action of the drama. Vautrin describes Paris as 'une forêt du Nouveau-Monde' (128) where every man is a hunter; Madame de Beauséant sees society as 'une réunion de dupes et de fripons' (94), with success as the only criterion; and the other characters are equally vehement in their judgment on the 'bourbier' of the city. There comes across most forcibly a sense of frenzied movement as the inhabitants, restless, ambitious, prodigal, pursue pleasure and fortune with no thought for the morrow or for morality. In their relationships to one another the characters can be divided into two main groups, the 'executioners' and the 'victims'; but the primary force with which all must contend is the 'Juggernaut' of contemporary society which threatens them with brutalization and destruction.

If the city is represented as an implacable machine, it is money which makes the wheels go round. Balzac, himself an indiscriminate spender, an unsound investor and a perpetual debtor, was appalled and fascinated by the triumphant rise of post-Napoleonic capitalism. His obsession with the almost limitless power of money and his curiosity about all aspects of financial activity are always in evidence, and it has been often suggested that the most dynamic element in his work, indeed the true hero of the *Comédie humaine*, is the 'pièce à cent sous'. In *Le Père Goriot* money is a unifying factor and a common denominator, and the general theme is constructed from scores of sharply observed details and suggestive transactions. Exact calculations permit the reconstruction of the dismal life of the boarders (dinner 30 francs a month, full pension 45 francs for Goriot and Michonneau). Mysterious nocturnal activities have pecuniary overtones: Goriot transforms his treasured possessions into marketable ingots, gold changes hands between Vautrin and his unknown visitor. There are notable examples of hoarding, spending and lending: Madame Vauquer has stealthily amassed 40,000 francs (roughly equivalent to £8,000 today), Goriot indulges in suspicious prodigality, and Vautrin, the outlaws' Nucingen, occasionally floats a short-term loan to the boarders. Later Mademoiselle Michonneau haggles over the price of a betrayal, Vautrin proposes Victorine as a solid investment, arranging a murder to prove his good faith, and Rastignac, having, like Delphine and Anastasie, 'bled' his family, is forced to draw on Vautrin's powerful resources to pay his gambling debts.

Once again the microcosmic boarding-house aptly foreshadows the world outside. Behind every Anastasie there is a Gobseck; Delphine and Nucingen are united by 'les chaînes d'or' (160). Vautrin is right as usual: his nightmarish vision of a Paris where wives are for sale and the rich commit crimes with impunity is confirmed by Delphine's conduct with de Marsay and by the grandiose schemes of her husband whose philosophy is based on a cynical *quid pro quo*:

Je te permets de commettre des fautes, laisse-moi faire des crimes en ruinant de pauvres gens! (254).

Moreover, an unbroken chain of gold links all the major characters in the novel. Rastignac is forced to gamble for Delphine to pay off de Marsay since Nucingen has 'invested' everything she received from her father; Goriot himself is powerless to help Anastasie who needs 12,000 francs to save Maxime; Rastignac, obligated to Delphine and Goriot for the new apartment, comes to the rescue by altering the figure on the promissory note received from Vautrin. And one by one the characters come to recognize that money alone unites master and slave in an almost indissoluble bond, and that wealth is the only universally respected value. Even Goriot, finally realizing that love will no longer draw his daughters to his bedside, urges Rastignac to tempt them with promises of financial reward: 'L'argent donne tout, même des filles' (289).

Rastignac, quick to profit from accumulating experience, begs, borrows and forges his way to success. The distance that separates him from the traditional hero is indicated by Delphine as she thrusts upon him the trappings of their new apartment:

> Autrefois les dames ne donnaient-elles pas à leurs chevaliers des armures, des épées, des casques, des cottes de mailles, des chevaux, afin qu'ils pussent aller combattre en leur nom dans les tournois? Eh bien! Eugène, les choses que je vous offre sont les armes de l'époque, des outils nécessaires à qui veut être quelque chose (237).

Balzac's nineteenth-century hero, as we have already learned from an earlier scene, prepares to do battle with a sack of gold in either hand (113).

Sudden possession of income results in an immediate transformation of the individual. On receiving from his parents a replenishment of funds, Rastignac's energy and confidence redouble; it is as if life is renewed within him. Balzac generalizes: 'Il se passe en lui [l'étudiant] des phénomènes inouïs: il veut tout et peut tout . . .' (112). Later in the novel when we are given a contrasting image of disintegration as Rastignac recklessly squanders his substance (172–3), there is again the indication that more than money is at stake. And this is certainly true in the case of Goriot whose life drains away as he desperately attempts to keep pace with his daughters' relentless demands. Money is not only the sign of success but the symbol of energy. Prodigality leads to a dispersal of vital forces; duration is achieved by prudent investment (Nucingen) or downright hoarding (Gobseck). In a world where wealth is a weapon of destruction and a means of survival, virtue consists in spending wisely. On an individual as well as a social level Gobsecks' observation is apt: 'L'or représente toutes les forces humaines' (II, 629).

Passion: La passion est toute l'humanité (I, 12)

Passion, like money, is a force which actively works upon Balzac's humanity, galvanizing, tyrannizing, destroying. In many instances it leads to a transformation of the individual, raising even the most humble to sudden splendour. The portrait of Victorine indicates a pale, sickly creature, passive and melancholy; love alone, remarks Balzac, would cause a redemptive quickening of life (21). Such a transformation does in fact later occur; Rastignac provokes in Victorine an 'explosion de sentiment' which causes a momentary radiance (177); in a subsequent scene her face is surrounded by an 'auréole de bonheur' (207). Goriot is similarly transfigured by emotion; from a dull-witted, self-absorbed automaton, he becomes, when his soul is filled with love for his daughters, illuminated by the passion which possesses him (57, 59 and especially 151). The vivid images used to depict these instances of fervour and devotion often have religious overtones ('auréole', 'infusion', 'voix d'un ange') or are accompanied by references to religious painting (207, 238); at such privileged moments the characters seem to move beyond their terrestrial condition and ascend towards a state of pure spirituality.

In *Louis Lambert*, where Balzac speculates at length on these and related psychic phenomena, there are two passages which illuminate both theory and technique. In the first the narrator summarizes an important aspect of Lambert's beliefs, according to which soul and body are represented in man by two separate but related beings:

> Il y aurait en nous deux créatures distinctes. Selon Swedenborg, l'ange serait l'individu chez lequel l'être intérieur réussit à triompher de l'être extérieur (X, 380).

Death alone can cause the permanent liberation of the 'être intérieur', but moments of extreme tension, produced by passion or volition, can effect a temporary victory of inner forces over the base matter of the corporeal machine. Lambert finds evidence of powers similar to those he himself possesses in the *Martyrologium* 'où sont contenus les faits les plus curieux sur l'abolition complète de la vie corporelle à laquelle l'homme peut arriver dans les paroxysmes de ses facultés intérieures' (X, 441). Balzac, like his hero, was fascinated by such manifestations of extreme spirituality, and he confers upon rare and isolated figures (among them Véronique Graslin, Madame Grandet, Madame de Mortsauf and Goriot) temporary states of transcendence. In Goriot's case, passion releases the imprisoned soul and triumphs over the gross physical envelope. A martyr to his love, he momentarily joins the company of the elect.

But Goriot's passion, like that of Balthazar Claës in *La Recherche de l'absolu* or that of Frenhofer in *Le Chef-d'œuvre inconnu*, is a complex amalgam of the selfless and the egoistical, the sublime and the grotesque, the creative and the disruptive. In *La Recherche de l'absolu* Balzac, illustrating his conviction that '*les extrêmes se touchent*' (V, 308), stresses the kinship between genius and vice (IX, 489); in both *Louis Lambert* and *Le Chef-d'œuvre inconnu* a connection is established between passion and madness. Goriot's love is endowed with a similar ambiguity. The passion which is implicitly compared to Christ's love for the world (238) is also equated with canine affection and the basest animality. Goriot fawns at Delphine's feet and rubs his head against her dress (239–40); he trails after his daughters, uncomplainingly accepting brutality and servitude. Vautrin's contemptuous description of those 'hommes à passions' who sacrifice everything to their vice is unjust as a total assessment of Goriot but it does strike home; Goriot himself is finally brought to confess the vicious element in his love for his daughters whom he considered his 'mistresses' (291). His passion, admirable in its moments of sublime self-lessness, is also undiscriminating, egocentric and, finally, disruptive.

A further perspective on Goriot's passion can be obtained by consider-ing the character of Madame Vauquer. Her pompous declaration 'la vie est dans les meubles' (241) reads like a parody of Goriot's 'ma vie, à moi, est dans mes deux filles' (150); and her grief at the general exodus of the boarders ('c'est la fin du monde') is a far cry from Goriot's final anguished vision of a world in ruins. Balzac adopts towards her a posi-tion of irony, not compassion; he describes her panic as representing 'la vraie douleur, une douleur profonde, la douleur causée par l'intérêt froissé' (243). In a sense the gap which separates Madame Vauquer from Goriot is a narrow one, for Balzac in his consideration of passion was aware of the proximity of the noble and the base, and indeed, as we have seen, he posits their co-existence in Goriot himself. But Madame Vauquer's total absorption with self and her tyranny over others make her irredeemably despicable; her example serves to point up what is undeniably admirable in Goriot.

Ennobling or degrading, violent emotion profoundly affects rational conduct and self-control. Even the poised and eloquent Madame de Beauséant is thrown into disarray by its 'despotism' (82) and rendered speechless (like Goriot and like Madame Vauquer) by its impact (280). In spite of the clear-sighted knowledge, which she imparts to Rastignac, that in the jungle of Paris victory belongs to the coldly calculating, and that genuine emotion should be disguised at all costs (93), she is unable to prevent her love for Ajuda from invading her thoughts and domin-ating her actions. Though remaining morally uncorrupted by her passion, she becomes blind to her lover's betrayal and vulnerable to the hostility of others. Vautrin, while recognizing in himself 'de ces im-menses abîmes, de ces vastes sentiments concentrés que les niais appellent des vices' (179), is more circumspect than Madame de Beauséant; and unlike the prodigal Goriot, he attempts to dominate his instincts and channel his passion into purposeful activity. He disguises violent im-pulses behind an impenetrable exterior; emotion is expressed obliquely, gestures are controlled. In the boarding-house where Goriot is un-guarded and vulnerable, Vautrin is inscrutable and discreet. It is only during his conversations with Rastignac and in the scene of his capture that he reveals the full extent of his passionate nature, though in the latter instance he rapidly succeeds in dominating his instinctive reactions and in regaining his self-control.

Maurice Bardèche dismisses Vautrin's capture as 'un incident technique' which 'ne comporte aucune leçon'.[1] One is tempted to conclude that Balzac found himself compelled to create a convenient means of eliminating a figure who, getting out of hand, was in danger of taking over the whole novel. But the scene occupies, I believe, a significant position in the thematic structure of the work. It anticipates the abdication of Madame de Beauséant and the death of Goriot, and it provides the basis for Rastignac's eventual recognition of the precariousness of Revolt (276). More immediately, Vautrin's heroic domination of self ('il se mit à sourire et regarda sa perruque' [222]) is a striking lesson for the impressionable Rastignac who, taunted moments later by Mademoiselle Michonneau, manages to restrain himself from physical violence: 'Rastignac se croisa les bras et resta muet' (228). The syntactical and rhythmical similarity of the two sentences drives home the parallelism between the situations, providing an insight into Rastignac's developing character.

Basically Rastignac is emotional and quick-tempered; Balzac describes him as having 'une de ces têtes pleines de poudre qui sautent au moindre choc' (114). Under pressure from Vautrin, he reacts with spontaneous indignation to compromising proposals; his rejection is based on sentiment rather than calculation: 'Je ne veux penser à rien, le cœur est un bon guide' (133). In his first encounter with Anastasie de Restaud he behaves with passionate abruptness, and his reactions on seeing Delphine at the theatre are those of a young man who wears his heart on his sleeve. On more than one occasion Madame de Beauséant chides him for his demonstrativeness (85, 141), and she urges him to feign indifference and disguise emotion; similar counsel is offered by Vautrin who warns Rastignac that 'il devait déposer à la barrière sa conscience, son cœur, mettre un masque, se jouer sans pitié des hommes' (138). In his relations with Goriot and Madame de Beauséant, Rastignac continues to demonstrate generosity and sensitivity; but his involvement with Delphine is a 'passion de commande' (153), and though he momentarily succumbs to a genuine passion which places him in an inferior position, he later redresses the balance and begins to gain ascendancy and move towards the possessive arrogance of the accomplished dandy. Rastignac joins Musset's Lorenzo and Stendhal's Julien in recognizing the value of dissembling; but whereas Lorenzo finally attempts to throw off stifling disguise and rediscover purity, and Julien recognizes that felicity can only be attained by surrender to the moment and to memory, Rastignac

[1] Maurice Bardèche, *Une Lecture de Balzac*, Paris, 1964, p. 109.

becomes enslaved by the mask he assumes. In the later novels which trace his brilliant social and political career, he is seen as a person of fixed characteristics, unregeneratively cynical and indifferent.

In demonstrating the multiple effects of passion on his characters, Balzac creates in *Le Père Goriot* an atmosphere of tension and violence. His scientific investigations led him to consider emotion not as an abstraction but as a substance or fluid of galvanizing power whose origins are uncertain and whose consequences are unpredictable. At times passion seems to have an existence independent of persons: it is a force which 's'empreint en toutes choses et traverse les espaces' (135). Balzac speaks of the 'contagion des sentiments' (114), of the 'affluence' of emotions (227), of the 'puissance d'infusion des sentiments' (151). His characters, subjected to this omnipresent force, are engaged in continuous warfare and a struggle for survival. Defeat attends those who fail to achieve lucidity or self-dominion; victory goes to the calculating and the unscrupulous, the capitalists of passion who exploit the feelings of others while retaining control over their own. Spontaneity, sensitivity and idealism are outmoded, profitless values. Rastignac, meditating, concludes for Balzac: 'Les belles âmes ne peuvent pas rester longtemps en ce monde. Comment les grands sentiments s'allieraient-ils, en effet, à une société mesquine, petite, superficielle?' (286).

Revolt: Tout ou rien! voilà ma devise (154)

Confronted by corruption and the destructive pressures of a mechanical existence, Balzac's characters are forced to make a choice and a decision; Vautrin, oversimplifying, indicates the alternatives: 'ou une stupide obéissance ou la révolte' (119). Madame de Beauséant, Goriot and Vautrin himself all take a stand in an attempt to rise above circumstances and to create and preserve an independent vision of reality. The aristocrat, the bourgeois and the criminal, though they inhabit spheres which seem to have little in common, are linked by their reactions to society and by their efforts to establish a world of their own making.

Madame de Beauséant would appear to have little reason for revolutionary fervour. In a society obsessed by rank and hierarchy, she occupies the uncontested position of 'queen' of the faubourg Saint-Germain; her denunciation of the world might initially be considered no more than a fashionable expression of contempt for the vulgar. But her castigation of society for its egoism and cruelty reveals a personal note of bitterness and a pessimism amounting almost to misanthropy, and her cynical and disillusioned advice to Rastignac is indicative of a heartfelt protest (93-4). The substance of her complaint is repeated in the less

articulate but equally despairing cries of Goriot who obscurely recognizes society's part in the denial of the claims of paternity and in the
corruption of his daughters (290–91).

Vautrin's attitude is the most extreme; rejecting contemporary
morality, law and justice, he reduces society to the lowest possible level
and expresses his view of it with devastating clarity:

> Voilà la vie telle qu'elle est. Ça n'est pas plus beau que la cuisine, ça
> pue tout autant, et il faut se salir les mains si l'on veut fricoter; sachez
> seulement vous bien débarbouiller: là est toute la morale de notre
> époque (125).

Such contemptuous and splenetic criticism was common enough in
Balzac's time; many of his contemporaries (Stendhal, Vigny, Musset,
for example) viewed their society with a similar mixture of cynicism
and disgust. Musset's Lorenzo expresses his despair in terms which recall
Vautrin:

> Je connais la vie, et c'est une vilaine cuisine, sois-en persuadé. Ne mets
> pas la main là-dedans, si tu respectes quelque chose (Lorenzaccio, III, iii).

But whereas Lorenzo convinces his companion of the futility of action,
and recognizes that commitment inevitably sullies and destroys, and
whereas Stendhal's heroes escape contamination only by withdrawal,
Vautrin urges upon Rastignac a descent into the arena and a ceaseless
participation which, however unidealistic, represents an assertion of self
and a denial of the inevitable: 'N'est-ce pas d'ailleurs une belle partie à
jouer que d'être seul contre tous les hommes et d'avoir la chance?' (118).
His conception of revolt, though egocentric and anarchical, is a dynamic
protest against inertia, submissiveness and the tyranny of history.

Balzac's major characters are basically extremists whose defiance goes
well beyond a rejection of social attitudes and patterns. Madame de
Beauséant, faced with the possibility of abandonment, refuses to accept
that her love can be less than eternal. Having glimpsed the ideal, she
attempts to perpetuate its presence; confronted with failure, she prefers
solitude to compromise. Goriot is afflicted by desire to transcend the
limits of space and time; obstinately refusing to accept the limitations
of the human condition, he revolts against the implacable process of life
itself. His wish to participate in the exotic existence of his daughters
results, on a literal level, in his plan to live close to Delphine and Rastignac so that he can come and go 'comme un bon esprit qui est partout'
(235). And this longing for omnipresence is translated into an urgent
plea to be granted the power to extend his protective vigil beyond
death: 'Dites donc, si je vais en paradis, je pourrai revenir sur terre en

esprit autour d'elles' (287). Vautrin's facile ubiquity seems like a parody of Goriot's desperate striving for immortality; his disguises and unpredictable appearances have much of the purely melodramatic about them. But in fact Vautrin is more than an extravagant jack-in-the-box. His attempt to replace chance by certainty, his promise to Rastignac of perpetual vigilance, his refusal to squander his resources and his assumption of limitless power indicate a repudiation of the contingent and a rejection of the claims of ordinary existence.

In pursuing their quest for victory over time and human frailty, both Goriot and Vautrin assume exalted rôles. Goriot's fanatical paternal drive causes him to compare himself to God, immanent in his creation:

> Enfin, je vis trois fois. Voulez-vous que je vous dise une drôle de chose? Eh bien! quand j'ai été père, j'ai compris Dieu. Il est tout entier partout, puisque la création est sortie de lui. Monsieur, je suis ainsi avec mes filles (151).

His existence is multiplied and perpetuated in his daughters; he lives and expresses himself through those whom he has created. Vautrin annexes similar powers: 'Moi, je me charge du rôle de la Providence, je ferai vouloir le bon Dieu' (130). But whereas Goriot seeks to lose himself in his creation, Vautrin attempts to impose his will on those whom he fashions in his own image. This urge for domination is evident in his trial of strength with Rastignac whom he wishes to manipulate as he pleases, and is made explicit in *Illusions perdues* during a conversation with Lucien de Rubempré:

> Je veux animer ma créature, la façonner, la pétrir à mon usage, afin de l'aimer comme un père aime son enfant (IV, 1032).

Vautrin towers above his creatures and while vicariously participating in their success remains separate from them, transcending the results of his handiwork.

It is possible to see in Goriot who loses himself in his creation and in Vautrin who attempts to remain committed but aloof a reflection of two major tendencies in Balzac's own creative activity. On the one hand, sympathetic participation and a knowledge which comes from passionate identification: 'devenir un autre que soi par l'ivresse des facultés morales', as he wrote in *Facino Cane* (VI, 67); on the other hand, imperious manipulation, arbitration, judgment and, if necessary, execution. Both these stances imply a revolutionary seizure of power which sets up man in competition with his own Creator; and Balzac, while giving in full measure the sublime aspects of this Promethean endeavour, does not fail to impart his awareness of its perils. Goriot, like Frenhofer in

Le Chef d'œuvre inconnu, falls victim to his own creation; uncritical surrender leads to inarticulateness and immolation. The successful creator must achieve distance between himself and his work in order to protect his capacity for ordering experience and to preserve his critical sense. The point is made clear in *Massimilia Doni*:

> Quand un artiste a le malheur d'être plein de la passion qu'il veut exprimer, il ne saurait la peindre, car il est la chose même au lieu d'en être l'image (IX, 381).

In this respect, the controlled and lucid Vautrin would seem to come closer to Balzac's ideal creator. A manipulator of persons who possesses uncanny powers of intuition and divination, an artist in crime who read Cellini, a 'poet' whose poetry consists of actions and emotions (126), he seems to represent an equilibrium between dictatorial aloofness and passionate involvement. And yet there are disquieting elements which have been too readily ignored by those who would make of Vautrin a reflection of Balzac himself. Even on a literal level, Vautrin lacks the omnipotence we have the right to expect from one who usurps the function of Providence. He does not know at first that Delphine and Anastasie are Goriot's daughters; he dismisses the notion that Goriot might be a police spy (35) but fails to realize that Michonneau is one, in spite of Bianchon's observation on her 'bosses de Judas' (63)! And he indirectly assures his own downfall by interrupting Rastignac's compromising talk with Victorine, by rendering Bianchon incapable of mentioning the reference to Trompe-la-Mort and by antagonizing Mademoiselle Michonneau. We may well agree with his own observation that 'La Providence a des voies bien cachées' (208)! Moreover, in Balzac's own case destructive satire is accompanied by affirmation through creativity and the establishment of enduring structures, whereas the Mephistophelian Vautrin, if not exactly 'der Geist der stets verneint', preaches a sterile hedonism and an anarchism which is close to the futile. The revelation of his homosexuality takes the grandeur out of his proud misogyny, and makes a mockery out of his defiant assertion 'je ne suis pas curieux de me replanter ici par bouture' (180). Finally his dream of absolute felicity turns out to be nothing more than the wish to live like a king surrounded by slaves on a large plantation in the U.S.A. Viewed in the light of this disproportion between theory and action, Vautrin remains, it seems to me, a complex mixture of Prometheanism and parody.

It is a common and valid thesis that Romanticism brought into favour a glorification of the creative potential of the individual who, by giving expression to forces discovered within him, participates in the process

of a world of dynamic movement and progressive change. Balzac undoubtedly shared in this revolutionary vision; his awareness of the
liberating effects of emotion and of the possibility of man's ascension to
higher states of being, his exaltation of the stature and function of the
artist, together with his own desire to set himself up as rival to Cuvier,
to Napoleon, even to God himself, make him a Promethean figure even
among his contemporaries. Hostile to inhibiting constriction and
mechanical patterns of thought and action, he asserted his independence
in grandiose terms: 'Je fais partie de l'opposition qui s'appelle la vie.'
And yet, unlike many of the Romantics, he clearly saw and expressed
the necessity, in society, passion and art, for the tempering of extremism
through discipline, for the structuring of the exuberant imagination and
for the achieving of harmony between cause and effect, act and goal.
Troubled, perhaps, by a sense of his own *démesure*, he forced himself to
recognize, even if many of his greatest characters do not, the limitations
imposed on man by nature, time and death.

Bildung: Les voies tortueuses ne mènent à rien de grand
(107)

From *Don Quixote* to Joyce's *Ulysses* the theme of the formative
journey has been a central preoccupation of fiction. Some novelists have
chosen to trace the total pattern of their hero's existence; others have
dwelt on a crucial stage in his development. Balzac's system of inter-
locking novels enables him to combine these two approaches: in *Le Père
Goriot* he concentrates on the initial steps in Rastignac's career which is
then developed in other works throughout the *Comèdie humaine*.

The action of *Le Père Goriot* occupies less than three months, and this
might seem too brief a span in which to speak of the formation of a
hero. And yet the intensity and compression of the events described and
the profound impact they make on Rastignac's character and outlook
compensate for the brevity of the experience. Naturally perspicacious,
Rastignac quickly succeeds in assimilating the lessons received and in
transforming knowledge into action; from a naïve and clumsy provincial he becomes, in the space of a few weeks, an experienced, agile
and disillusioned man of the world. Though his youthful dreams are
demolished by the nightmare of Paris, he is able to generate the necessary
force to preserve himself, if not from contamination, at least from total
defeat.

Balzac does not content himself with an unimpassioned charting of
Rastignac's journey. Whereas he tends to remain exterior to the other
characters, he enters the mind of his hero, dramatizing the movement of
intelligence and conscience. Moreover, he does not hesitate to make

comments on Rastignac's progress, to pass judgment and to generalize from the particular instance. A pattern emerges here: experience, meditation, commentary. Rastignac, subjected to a test, reflects upon his performance; the author then surveys and judges both achievement and assessment. There is a sense of progression, evaluation and unification: isolated events and themes are drawn together by the experience of the hero and the commentary of the narrator. Rastignac is brought into contact with the other major characters while the focus remains on his thoughts and actions. A study of the variants reveals that the majority of the lengthy additions to the original manuscript are concerned primarily with Rastignac and his 'education' (e.g. pp. 40, 173, 243-8). Originally Balzac had named his hero de Massiac, but Rastignac (who had made already an appearance in La Peau de chagrin) was substituted on page 43 of the manuscript, and he steadily increases in importance until he finally becomes the unifying factor in the total structure of the novel.

At the outset Rastignac tends towards reverie rather than ratiocination, and his path leads him into illusion, error and collision. On his return to the boarding-house after his first ball (at which he had distinguished himself by his ignorance), Rastignac, day-dreaming, transforms a hesitant beginning into an achieved success (43-6). The narrator, while sympathizing with his hero ('qui n'aurait comme Eugène . . . ?'), indicates the part played by imagination, and corrects distorted impressions ('le naïf étudiant', 'Rastignac crut', etc.). Returning to Madame de Beauséant's, Rastignac again surrenders to reverie; Balzac inserts a general comment on young men at this stage of life:

> Ils ne calculent alors ni les obstacles ni les dangers, ils voient en tout le succès, poétisent leur existence par le seul jeu de leur imagination, et se font malheureux ou tristes par le renversement de projets qui ne vivaient encore que dans leurs désirs effrénés (67).

These youthful Don Quixotes, sublimely self-confident and blind to actuality, begin their journey having already 'arrived'. But reality, as immediately becomes apparent, remains obdurately present, ready to take revenge. Rastignac, day-dreaming, becomes spattered with mud, and, a few moments later in the Restaud's house, enraged by the mocking servants, he stumbles over the furniture and almost falls into the bath-tub. It is significant that these two incidents are immediately followed by the brief scene, observed by Rastignac, in which Goriot, leaving the house, is almost crushed to death beneath the wheels of his son-in-law's carriage. The sanctions imposed seem harsh, but their implication is clear: retreat into dream or desire leads to vulnerability and a brutal awakening.

Rastignac emerges here as a potential Goriot, beset by illusions, passionately self-absorbed. His 'désirs effrénés' impair his vision and prevent him from giving attention to the reality which confronts him. We observe a similar loss of focus in the following scene when Madame de Beauséant, disturbed by her passion for Ajuda, begins by ignoring Rastignac's presence, and even after being jolted out of her self-absorption later addresses him by the wrong name. All Balzac's creatures of sentiment are apt to see things through an imperfect and distorting lens; their imagination creates an image which they superimpose on the world and to which they expect reality to conform. They move in a trance, unpreoccupied with the paraphernalia of everyday existence; and Balzac has made it plain during his descriptions of décor that in modern life objects are a force to be reckoned with! Inattentive to the remarks of others, neglectful, in some instances, of clothes and appearance, these inspired somnambulists fix their gaze on the future and feed on their visions.

Undoubtedly Rastignac bears (and to some extent deserves to bear) a charmed life. His cousin's name is a 'talisman' which grants protection and power, Goriot's 'magic wand' transforms a shabby room in the boarding-house into a luxurious apartment in the rue d'Artois, and a 'miracle' prevents the triumph of Vautrin's grand designs. But this atmosphere of the *Arabian Nights* is accompanied by the unsettling reality of a hostile environment. Rastignac's journey which in his imagination he envisioned as a magical ascent turns into an obstacle race; traps are baited, doors are closed in his face, objects are set in his path. His first task (which is that of all successful travellers in the *Comédie humaine*) is to pay attention to the present and to learn to negotiate the furniture.

Rastignac assimilates this early lesson and, profiting from advice and example, moves resolutely but cautiously towards his desired goal. At the end of the novel 'victory' is in sight, but the cost has still to be assessed. Against attainment of lucidity, understanding of the world and achievement of social success must be set loss of purity, abandonment of morality, defeat of revolutionary fire. The world is conquered, but Rastignac's soul is irremediably tarnished. And although he has succeeded in learning to live in the present, he discovers that in doing so he has ruptured connections with the past:

[Il se voyait] si loin du Rastignac venu l'année dernière à Paris, qu'en le lorgnant par un effet d'optique morale, il se demandait s'il se ressemblait en ce moment à lui-même (246).

With regard to his family his 'optique morale' has undergone a transformation; initially he considered family life petty and restrictive, later it takes on a different aspect:

> Il se souvint des pures émotions de cette vie calme, il se rappela les jours passés au milieu des êtres dont il était chéri. En se conformant aux lois naturelles du foyer domestique, ces chères créatures y trouvaient un bonheur plein, continu, sans angoisses (276).

Like Goriot, who looks forever backwards to the 'paradise' of his daughters' childhood in the rue de la Jussienne, Rastignac can now discover felicity only in an unattainable past. Living only for the present, placing his trust in the pleasure of the moment, he has forfeited the possibility of discovering plenitude and permanence. Rejecting solitude he has discovered isolation: 'Moi, je suis en enfer, et il faut que j'y reste' (283).

Rastignac's final position, though explicable by the context of the work, is not, however, seen as inevitable; Balzac comments:

> S'il est des exceptions à ces lois draconiennes du code parisien, elles se rencontrent dans la solitude, chez les âmes qui ne se sont point laissé entraîner par les doctrines sociales, qui vivent près de quelque source aux eaux claires, fugitives, mais incessantes (245).

In *Le Père Goriot*, and indeed in the whole of the *Comédie humaine*, such an ideal is rarely attained. Bianchon in this novel, d'Arthez and the members of the Cénacle in *Illusions perdues*, are among the few who redeem the rest of Balzac's humanity. Triumphing over the egoism and corruption of their century, refusing to be driven by passion or lust for gold, they direct their energy towards goals in harmony with their talents and their idealism. A perspective is achieved which includes the full recognition of the present without sacrificing the claims of memory or the exigencies of the future. Avoiding the absolutist positions of a Goriot or a Vautrin, they go beyond the compromise elected by Rastignac, searching, like Balzac himself, for a reconciliation which permits creative action.

4. Images

Introducing, in the garden of the boarding-house, the scaly statue of Love, Balzac makes a passing reference to symbol-hunters who might be tempted to transform a shabby reality into myth (8). It is hard to say whether the remark is a challenge or a warning; many of Balzac's recent critics, at all events, have chosen the former interpretation, and they have responded by rejecting the nineteenth-century conception of Balzac as social realist in favour of a view of him as poet, visionary and creator of myths. Following several illustrious predecessors, Maurice Bardèche in his most recent book[1] places the emphasis firmly on Balzac's imaginative vision, and bids us enter the *Comèdie humaine* by way of the *Etudes philosophiques.*

Bardèche tends perhaps to make too neat a pattern out of the grand diversity of Balzac's universe; but his focus is penetrating and he succeeds in providing a superb sense of the unity of the *Comédie humaine.* We do well to remember that from *Sténie* to *La Peau de chagrin* speculation preceded and informed creation; and the latter work (of which Balzac wrote 'tout y est mythe et figure') undoubtedly provides the key to much of what was later to become the *Comédie humaine.* Written in an exuberant, imagistic style, *La Peau de chagrin* explores many of Balzac's major obsessions, and bodies forth his vision of the drama of human existence expressed in terms of energy and will. We have already considered the impact of these theories on the action of the novel and on the tempo and pattern of the individual life. It should be remembered that Balzac considered thought and passion a material substance which can be observed and analysed; indeed he optimistically anticipated scientific confirmation of his speculations:

> Peut-être le jour n'est-il pas loin où l'on saisira le mode par lequel le sentiment se condense chimiquement en un fluide, peut-être pareil à celui de l'électricité (V, 1092).

Lack of incontrovertible proof did not prevent Balzac from exploiting his theories: time and again he describes the movement and transmission of emotion in physical terms (compression, expansion, emanation, projection, collision), and shows its effect on the physiognomy of his characters. This dramatization of forces is often expressed by metaphors

[1] Maurice Bardèche, *Une Lecture de Balzac,* Paris, 1964.

and similes of a direct and substantial nature; imagery translates a fanciful vision into the reality of language.

When emotion is generated or received, it is frequently expressed as physical sensation; the organism reacts to the flux of forces. Popular metaphors and Romantic clichés abound: jealousy 'devours' (93), remorse 'gnaws' (174), entrails 'burn' (294), hearts are 'rent' by claws of steel (132), emotional 'daggers' plunge (87). The thirty or so images of this type, stark and unoriginal, are briskly exploited; Balzac rejects subtlety in favour of directness. These figures of speech are sporadically employed except during Goriot's agony where they accumulate (thirteen examples in thirty pages). Here they become effective: used by Goriot himself, their direct simplicity is moving. The disintegration of the mind is portrayed by metaphors of burning and compression; the heart is torn asunder by the violent force of passion. Imagery points up the polarity between thought and emotion; Goriot, here as throughout, is a creature of sentiment, indifferent, indeed hostile to ratiocination: 'Coupez-moi la tête, laissez-moi seulement le cœur' (294). And our final vision of him is in keeping with this pattern; even after his mind has almost entirely ceased to function, we witness '[le] terrible éclat d'une force de sentiment qui survivait à la pensée' (301). His passion, recorded on his physiognomy, triumphs over the mechanism it destroys.

Sentiments and ideas, which may become self-defeating, can also be projected from one individual to another with, at times, devastating effect. Balzac makes this clear in a long metaphorical passage on page 114, which reads in part:

> Sans doute les idées se projettent en raison directe de la force avec laquelle elles se conçoivent, et vont frapper là où le cerveau les envoie, par une loi mathématique comparable à celle qui dirige les bombes au sortir du mortier.

Certain temperaments are able to resist, others are more vulnerable and are destroyed by the forces to which they are subjected. Taken literally such theories may seem to have more in common with science-fiction than science; but while questioning their accuracy, we can still admire their expressive and dramatic value. Vautrin's mysterious power over others is emphatically demonstrated by his glance; through a process of intensification ('regard divinateur', 'regard froidement fascinateur', 'regard magnétique'), Balzac builds up the terrible reality of his character. In Goriot's case it is the glance received which is significant: his joy, dependent on the light projected by his daughters, is extinguished by its absence: 'Depuis le jour où leurs yeux n'ont plus rayonné sur moi, j'ai toujours été en hiver ici' (292). In all, some forty images are connected with the *regard*; at times whole scenes are played out by means of gesture and glance. The characters are constantly 'reading' signs, interpreting countenances, intercepting or deflecting the *regard* of others; there is an overall sense of intellectual and emotional warfare.

Inner forces are everywhere revealed by expression, action and gesture. Here again Balzac is often content to rely on traditional modes of expression ('la comtesse pâlit d'abord . . . puis elle rougit') and conventional metaphors ('les yeux de la veuve s'allumèrent'). But there is a dominant group of images, connected with heat and light and grounded in Balzac's view of emotion as substance or fluid, which take on individuality through their intensity, repetition and application. Victorine, filled with joy by her love for Rastignac, becomes surrounded by an 'auréole du bonheur' (207); Rastignac himself, at a moment of crisis, 's'était embelli de son désespoir, et resplendissait de tous les feux de l'enfer qu'il avait au cœur' (193). The latter image is taken up again and developed at some length during the scene of Vautrin's capture (222–3); the former is also expanded, and used to portray the sublimity of Goriot's passion (151). The passage is worth quoting in full:

Le père Goriot était sublime. Jamais Eugène ne l'avait pu voir illuminé par les feux de sa passion paternelle. Une chose digne de remarque est la puissance d'infusion que possèdent les sentiments. Quelque grossière que soit une créature, dès qu'elle exprime une affection forte et vraie, elle exhale un fluide particulier qui modifie la physionomie, anime le geste, colore la voix. Souvent l'être le plus stupide arrive, sous l'effort de la passion, à la plus haute éloquence dans l'idée, si ce n'est dans le language, et semble se mouvoir dans une sphère lumineuse. Il y avait en ce moment dans la voix, dans le geste de ce bonhomme, la puissance communicative qui signale le grand acteur. Mais nos beaux sentiments ne sont-ils pas les poésies de la volonté?

The splendour of this moment has to some extent been anticipated by other images pointing up the contrast between Goriot's habitual lacklustre appearance and his reactions to news of his daughters. The moment is none the less striking in its intensity. Balzac moves conventionally enough from statement to demonstration, but he achieves his effect through a startling fusion of the literal and the metaphorical. Here, as throughout the novel, imagery bridges the gap between the prosaic and the miraculous. The characters, at such moments, remain as we have known them and yet achieve a new and unexpected dimension.

*

Images are also used by Balzac to deform his characters, to criticize and to judge them. A recent study of the 120 animal images in *Le Père*

Goriot reveals the extent of Balzac's pessimism with regard to the majority of his characters.[1] The process of dehumanization is intensified, in certain instances, by the equation of human beings with objects: 'mécanique' (19), 'pivot' (20), 'squelette' (18), etc. A comic note (bordering on the grotesque) is sometimes introduced by the narrator when describing the antics of his minor characters: Poiret's words drip from his lips like water from a tap (191); Madame Vauquer is roasted by desire 'comme une perdrix dans sa barde' (28); Mademoiselle Michonneau reacts to a suggestive remark of Vautrin's like 'un cheval de régiment entendant le son de la trompette', and a moment later lowers her eyes 'comme une religieuse qui voit des statues' (58). At a crucial point in the life of Madame Vauquer (when she is faced with the general exodus of the boarders), Balzac metes out punishment in a rather heavy-handed manner:

> La vieille hôtesse était là comme Marius sur les ruines de Carthage. . . . Quoique lord Byron ait prêté d'assez belles lamentations au Tasse, elles sont bien loin de la profonde vérité de celles qui échappaient à madame Vauquer (240).

Here the humour is provided by deliberate overstatement and by setting up an obvious disproportion between the comparison and the character. Balzac seems to be parodying his own predilection for hyperbole.

The major part of the comic relief is, of course, supplied by Vautrin whose rich, pungent and ferocious figures of speech enliven the sombre atmosphere of the boarding-house. His wit is pointed, ironical, derogatory: the boarding-house is 'une vertueuse mansarde' (172), Madame Vauquer in her finery is 'ficelée comme une carotte' (208), the treacherous Michonneau is 'cagnotte', 'curieuse' (224), 'vieille vendeuse de chair' (225). Vautrin confirms his multifarious background by fashioning images from a wide range of experience and activity—military, nautical, legal, literary, hunting, criminal, gambling, etc. In his first long monologue (118–32) he overwhelms Rastignac by a veritable explosion of images (almost a hundred in fifteen pages!), and in the speech after his capture, he reveals his true origins by a succession of violent metaphors based on popular expressions and criminal slang. Like Balzac, Vautrin does not shun the overworked image and the cliché (there are seven on pages 121–3), but he frequently coins expressions which support his claim to originality. To kill oneself is 'aller flâner dans les filets de Saint-Cloud' (119), the dandy becomes 'l'homme en gants et à paroles jaunes' (132), Gobseck is described as 'capable de faire des dominos avec les os de

[1] See Léon-François Hoffman, 'Les Métaphores Animales dans *Le Père Goriot*' in *L'Année balzacienne* (1963), pp. 91–103.

son père' (52)! Direct, brutal, satirical, Vautrin's images destroy illusions and reduce existence to the level of anarchy and animality; it is he who most aptly and succinctly sums up the lesson of Balzac's Paris: 'Il faut vous manger les uns les autres comme des araignées dans un pot . . .' (124).

Other characters are less vigorously articulate, yet each of the persons in the novel is endowed with a particular mode of expression; Balzac is attentive to levels of language and personal idiosyncrasies of diction and vocabulary. There is, first of all, a linguistic stratification which corresponds to social position. Christophe and Sylvie, for example, use the most rudimentary kinds of similes in keeping with their semi-popular idiom: 'dur comme du fer' (49), 'dorment comme des souches' (50), 'c'est comme un dogue' (241), etc. Madame de Beauséant's figures of speech, as is to be expected, are mostly of a complex and sophisticated nature (see pp. 93-4), though both she and the duchesse de Langeais are capable of using metaphorical expressions which startle by their brutal directness (see pp. 90-1). Balzac also shows a concern for the relationship between language and occupation; like Diderot he recognized the influence exerted by profession on outlook and speech (Avant-Propos, I, 5).[1] Bianchon, in Le Père Goriot, sees Goriot as a 'fait médical' (66), and many of his observations, some humorous, some serious, are expressed in images based on natural history or medicine (p. 63, etc.).

Above all, direct speech reveals the particularity of individual persons, and here again it is through imagery that a characteristic note is sounded. Madame Vauquer's pretentiousness is brought out when she replaces Sylvie's incorrect use of 'patron-jacquette' by the equally improper 'patron-minette' (50); Gondureau's pun on 'homme de marque' (186) points up his grimly sardonic nature; and Sylvie's comment on Poiret and Michonneau ('ils sont tous deux si secs que, s'ils se cognent, ils feront feu comme un briquet' [60]) momentarily breaks the stereotype. In the case of Goriot, an early image draws attention to his passionate obstinacy and suggests an elemental, animal nature: 'J'aimerais mieux gratter la terre avec mes ongles que de me séparer de cela' (27). At times, appropriately, he expresses his affection in flowery and sentimental figures ('oyant gazouiller vos enfants' [150]), and he constantly makes reference to angels, God, the Trinity, paradise and hell, even going to the extent of comparing his last kiss to the sacrament (292). It is the sacrilegious rather than the sacred that is striking here; the lack of discrimination reveals ignorance, and blind egoism. And yet even though Goriot's

[1] For the influence of profession on speech in Diderot and Balzac, see Jean Pommier, 'Comment Balzac relaie Diderot' in Revue des Sciences Humaines (April–September 1951), pp. 161-6.

language in general shows an absence of rigour, maturity and taste (he himself admits on page 150 that he is unable to put two words together), it is by no means devoid of energy and verve, even originality. His description of Nucingen as 'une tête de veau sur un corps de porc' (198), his use of such expressions as the neologism 'gobichonner' (233), his perspicacious self-evaluation as 'un méchant cadavre dont l'âme est partout où sont mes filles' (136), the accumulating violence of such verbs as 'guillotiner' (253), 'déchiqueter' (257), 'dévorer' (258), and the images he finds to express his final apocalyptic vision of the world (291), go well beyond the mechanical patterns of language which he habitually employs. We may not agree with Castex's view that at moments Goriot's diction makes us think of Lear (note on page 291), but it is undeniable that Balzac has succeeded in creating a language which vividly translates the peculiar dual nature of his hero.

*

The individual character is thus made present and evaluated by means of descriptive imagery and a diction charged with idiosyncratic figures of speech. Major themes are also underscored by a complex network of metaphor and simile, and there is a group of spatial images which contribute significantly to the meaning and the structure of the novel. Rastignac's journey, represented on a literal level as a succession of forays, setbacks and conquests, is charted and assessed by passages of analysis reinforced by images indicating situation and progress—'carrefour' (123), 'bagatelles de la porte' (182), 'barrière' (236), 'Rubicon' (245). His precarious path is a 'tight-rope' (45) stretched across social and moral abysses (76, 77, 134, 236). At the outset, goal, tempo and direction are determined: Rastignac resolves to 'launch' himself into society (41) in search of conquest and fortune. Distances are not measured, nor risks calculated; imagination suppresses the gap between expectation and fulfilment. Desire to succeed *becomes* success: 'Sa pensée vagabonde escomptait si drûment ses joies futures qu'il se croyait auprès de madame de Restaud' (46). For a moment it is as if Rastignac's course will take on the passionate fixity of that of a Goriot; his ardent meridional temperament and his driving ambition bring him close to Balzac's blind and unrelenting seekers of the absolute. But Rastignac's first testing day in Parisian society, with its rebuffs, warnings and exhortations to prudence, causes hesitation and re-evaluation; he gradually becomes aware of the merits of surveying, assessing, scrutinizing, measuring. Metaphorical expressions spatialize the psychological process: Rastignac resolves to 'connaître son échiquier' (101), learns to '[mesurer] le vaste champ qui s'ouvrait à ses regards' (153), to '[mesurer] la portée de sa position'

(170). He moves towards the attainment of a certain perspective on himself and his actions and the awareness of the obstacles which occupy the distance between present and future. Although in this novel he never reaches the 'point d'où l'homme peut contempler le cours de la vie et la juger' (245), the final scene, with its symbolism of height and vantage point, indicates a measure of success.

Throughout the novel spatial images are also used to indicate lines of force and patterns of morality. Alternative 'trajectories' are suggested to Rastignac by Vautrin: 'Il faut entrer dans cette masse d'hommes comme un boulet de canon, ou s'y glisser comme une peste' (124). Vautrin, the man of energy and resolution, urges the former course, the way of revolt: 'Vous, si vous êtes un homme supérieur, allez en *droite ligne* et la tête haute' (125). But the cautious and circumspect Rastignac finally chooses the path of indirection; he becomes as supple as an eel (146), expending energy with prudence, following the undulating pattern traced out in *La Peau de chagrin*. In the process, Rastignac 'enlarges' his conscience (95), compromises his ideals, and adapts his conduct to the prevailing ethic. Here he does follow Vautrin's advice as to the shape of the *moral* path to be taken:

> Un homme qui se vante de ne jamais changer d'opinion est un homme qui se charge d'aller toujours en *ligne droite*, un niais qui croit à l'infaillibilité (130).

In spite of his moments of compassion and resolve, Rastignac, morally corrupted by Vautrin, deviates from the ideal of rectitude illustrated, according to the narrator, by 'ces belles volontés qui ne se plient jamais au mal, à qui la moindre déviation de la *ligne droite* semble être un crime' (147). Indeed Rastignac's total performance is well described by Balzac as 'la peinture des *sinuosités* dans lesquelles un homme du monde, un ambitieux fait rouler sa conscience' (148). Renouncing both revolt and integrity, Rastignac gains success at the expense of heroism. The zigzag pattern of his outward path admirably symbolizes the inner hesitations, oscillations and compromises; and the conflict between ambition and morality is intensified and generalized by the series of corresponding figures of speech.

The world in which Rastignac learns to operate is, like the total world of the *Comédie humaine*, composed of groups, coteries and strata. One of the tasks undertaken by hero and narrator in *Le Père Goriot* is the exploration of the 'superposition des couches humaines qui composent la société' (40). It quickly becomes apparent that Balzac is interested not only in social hierarchy but also in all levels of human activity. At the base is the 'société complète' of the boarding-house, which comes to represent moral as well as social attitudes, the bestial and the degraded. Above is the 'cercle supérieur où brillaient les constellations' (158), that other society which, when thoroughly known, loses its brilliance and reveals itself as an 'océan de boue' (276), similar in kind to the world of the boarding-house. Beyond lies the dream-world inhabited by Madame de Beauséant, Goriot and Vautrin ('je vis dans une sphère plus élevée que celles des autres hommes' [180]); here too illusion plays a major rôle and the awakening is bitter. Finally, less in evidence but more enduring, is a circumscribed sphere of simple activity represented by Rastignac's family and by the modest Bianchon whose philosophy has about it a sense of proportion and harmony lacking in the others:

> Les affections de l'homme se satisfont dans le plus petit cercle aussi pleinement que dans une immense circonférence (156).

Those whose ambitions are too vast only succeed in dissipating their energy; force is centripetally dispersed instead of being channelled into a sphere of activity whose scope must be in keeping with one's abilities.

The basic geometry of *Le Père Goriot* (and of the *Comédie humaine* itself) can be seen as a series of lines and circles: individual destinies and spheres of activity, interest, influence. The lines vary according to fixity of purpose, directness of ascent and curve of fortune; they may threaten the circles, destroy them or become assimilated by them. On the human plane the circles are composed of groups of persons who are brought together by chance, philosophy, inertia, or desire for mutual protection. In some instances the units are horizontal, built along the social axis; others are vertical, cutting through lines of class. The interaction of these groups and the impact of individual destinies upon them form a major element in the structure of Balzac's novels.

*

There is, in *Le Père Goriot*, a very conscious application of metaphor and simile for purposes of prediction, confirmation and summation. Early in the novel, as we have already seen, Balzac injects a sense of inevitability into his drama by indicating that the events to be related have already taken place; the future, like the past, holds no secrets that have not already been uncovered. Goriot's death, for example, is prefigured in an image on the second page; he is to become the victim of inhuman forces:

> Le char de la civilisation, semblable à celui de l'idole de Jaggernat, à peine retardé par un cœur moins facile à broyer que les autres ... l'a brisé bientôt et continue sa marche glorieuse.

This particular figure of speech does more than anticipate later events; it provides the basis for a series of metaphors and similes which, strategically positioned throughout the novel, underline a major source of conflict. The view of the world of men as a brutal machine inhabited by automata is taken up in images used by Rastignac (147) and Vautrin (180) and in the description of the boarders (24); Goriot, by contrast, continues to be characterized in terms of his emotions and finally becomes stripped of extrinsic matter and reduced to a brave heart prepared for suffering and sacrifice:

' . . . mon cœur est grand, il peut tout recevoir. Oui, vous aurez beau le percer, les lambeaux feront encore des cœurs de père' (258-9).

The violence committed against him by society and by his daughters comes to a head in a crescendo of images: 'broyer' and 'briser' are echoed by '[tenailler] comme des bourreaux' (291), '[déchirer] le cœur' (272), 'marcher sur le cadavre' (292). And the Juggernaut, having claimed its victim, does, as predicted, continue along its inhuman path; the two worlds, boarding-house and society, totally indifferent to the death of Goriot, resume their life of egoism and pleasure. No other outcome, indeed, ever seemed possible; the action of the novel, itself an implacable mechanism, has moved inexorably towards an inevitable conclusion.

The image as *motif* is also exploited to recapitulate the past; Balzac makes frequent use of summarizing paragraphs in which he amasses a collection of figures of speech previously used in isolation. On pages 245-6, for example, a lengthy 'progress report' on Rastignac reads like a catalogue of Balzac's favourite images. The basic oppositions of the passage are between corruption and purity, change and permanence, egoism and altruism. Society, as so frequently, is seen as a battleground ('lice du monde'), and love as a religion (*v.* p. 172). Rastignac's desire to succeed is rendered as 'fièvre' and 'soif' (*v.* pp. 45, 121). At this point he has finally 'dépouillé sa peau d'homme de province' (*v.* p. 40), and he is able to discover his former self with difficulty, 'en se lorgnant par un effet d'optique morale' (*v.* p. 114). Permanence can be found only among those 'angelic' creatures who live in simple piety, a statement which recalls the terms of Rastignac's former references to his family (99) and to his sister (111). The equation of purity with 'quelque source aux eaux claires' contrasts sharply with Vautrin's earlier image of those 'hommes à passions' who are condemned to quench their thirst with the murky water drawn from the fountain of corruption (58). The casual reader may well not be struck by some of these echoes; but Balzac, at all events, was not a casual writer, and his use of imagery (particularly

when examined in the light of his corrections and additions) demonstrates his desire to impose a unity on the diversity of his material. He
works from the simple to the complex, from the isolated figure to the
general pattern; we witness, in his use of metaphor and simile, an
imagination perpetually struggling towards a final synthesis.

Stendhal once maliciously remarked that Balzac's novels seem to have
been written in two stages; initially the plot was constructed and then
the work was decorated with such lavish tropes as 'les pâtiments de
l'âme, il neige dans mon cœur, et autres belles choses'. The uncharitable
observation is a shrewd comment on Balzac's method of composition—
at least as regards the procedure adopted. A study of the variants shows
the extent to which Balzac relied on metaphor and simile in his numerous
additions to the original manuscript. At times he simply tacks on an
image to an existing phrase: 'je pleurais *comme une bête*' (61[g]); '[Poiret]
parlait toujours, *à l'instar d'une mécanique montée*' (192[a]), etc. More often
he expands a figurative expression already adumbrated: 'Je vous donne
mon nom comme un fil d'Ariane *pour entrer dans ce labyrinthe*' (94[j]; see
also 97[f], 128[e] and 151[k]). These additions and expansions usually serve to
intensify rather than to nuance. Moreover, the added image often con-
nects with a figure of speech already employed elsewhere: 'sphère
lumineuse' (151[k]) recalls the numerous metaphors of light used to
express emotion; 'ce labyrinthe' (94[j]) is an echo of 'labyrinthe parisien'
(40). Re-reading his work, Balzac admires an existing image and decides
to repeat it, expand it or create a variation upon it. Mademoiselle
Michonneau as 'Vénus du Père-Lachaise' strikes his fancy; her companion
subsequently receives a compensating promotion—'Apollon-Poiret',
'Mars-Poiret' (231)!

These superimposed images are often obviously intended to hammer
home a major theme, for example the explicit reference to 'bourreau'
and 'victime' (93), Bianchon's phrenological diagnosis of Goriot as 'un
Père *Eternel*' (97), the repetition of 'bourbier' to characterize Paris (60),
and the additions to the already crowded section of military images
(e.g. pp. 124, 138, 142, 176, 180). Other more striking insertions are
Vautrin's fearsome description of the struggle for survival (in the added
passage on page 124), Goriot's self-portrait as 'un méchant cadavre dont
l'âme est partout où sont mes filles' (136[h]), and the comments of Vautrin
on the 'depths' of his own being and on the strength of his resistance
(180[a]). There is a remarkable impression of welding in all this; we witness the attempt to increase the intensity and design of the novel by the
insertion of strategically positioned rivets. Balzac builds and reinforces,
labouring incessantly to expand the basic structure without sacrificing
its original force. Additions continued to appear in every edition of the

work; even his own copy of the Furne edition bears upon it modifications and interpolations for eventual incorporation.

★

There are just over 1,250 metaphors and similes in *Le Père Goriot*—about 5·3 per page in the Pléiade edition. A comparison with *Madame Bovary* (1·2 per page) or with *A la recherche du temps perdu* (1 per page) indicates the extraordinary density of Balzac's images. Their distribution through the work is irregular, but there is a general tendency towards a decrease in frequency (6·0 per page in the first chapter, 3·0 per page in Chapter IV), a tendency which is in keeping with the accelerating tempo of the action and the processes of excoriation and spoliation.

In the opening pages of the novel the description of décor is carried forward and organized in language which though far from neutral contains relatively few metaphorical expressions. The first massing of images occurs in the portraits; Balzac begins to reach out for hyperbole as he bodies forth his fantastic collection of creatures. From this point on the general movement of the work is like that of a heavy sea close to shore: an incessant ground-swell interspersed with sudden ejaculations of spray. Moments of comparative quiescence, as facts are marshalled and the narrative is pushed forward, are broken up by irruptions of figurative language which bring characters and events into sharp relief. The reader is forced to shift perspective and contemplate new and startling forms. The effect achieved, Balzac returns to a relatively sober and straightforward narrative style (as, for example, in the pages following Vautrin's capture). This 'Dämpfung' is particularly noticeable at the end of the work: the six pages between Goriot's death and Rastignac's final words contain only half a dozen figurative expressions. Throughout the novel, Balzac shows a clear preference for metaphor over simile (85 to 15 per cent). Unlike Flaubert who works skilfully with lengthy similes and whose elaborate and polished figures of speech are often to be admired for their own sake, Balzac frequently uses short, pungent images many of which come from the language of everyday conversation and depend for their effect not so much on their intrinsic beauty as on their appropriateness, forcefulness, positioning and repetition.

Balzac sets his imprint on everything he approaches; even the most commonplace materials are forged into extraordinary shapes and patterns. His imagination, elemental and poetic, expresses itself with immediacy through reference and analogy; his glance, capable of a steady focus on the forms of the external world, simultaneously penetrates beyond, discovering dark forces, hidden truths, unexpected illuminations. This double vision is synthesized by means of metaphorical

D

language: the exterior world is heightened and transformed, the realm of the spirit is materialized and made present. Imagery thus becomes more than a precarious middle term between extreme positions; it is the constant, unifying heart of Balzac's creative process.

5. Rhetoric

'Le narrateur est tout' (XI, 180)

The modern reader, accustomed to stories which 'tell themselves' or to novels which take place within the confines of a single consciousness, tends to regard the intrusive omniscient narrator with condescension, even with scorn. Our relativism makes us suspicious of the all-seeing creator who does not attempt to disguise his presence or withhold his judgment. Flaubert, James and their critics (especially these last) have extinguished what Sterne called the 'sunshine' of the novel; authorial digressions, generalizations and commentaries are out of favour.

Protests, fortunately, have been made. Wayne C. Booth, in his *Rhetoric of Fiction* (Chicago, 1961) has come forward with a spirited and reasoned defence of explicit authorial control, and he provides us with a solid study of 'the rhetorical resources available to the writer of epic, novel, or short story as he tries, consciously or unconsciously, to impose his fictional world upon the reader'.[1] We do well to remember that even in the most 'objective' work, the reader is always guided, however imperceptibly, towards some truth about experience, and the narrator adopts one or more of many stances in order to achieve his aim. Flaubert, for the most part, chooses to keep his presence discreetly disguised; Stendhal delights in playing a sophisticatedly ironic game of hide and seek with the reader. Balzac, even in his most modest moments, is always close to the stage; and for much of the time he bestrides his world like a Colossus, playing the parts of showman, propagandist, manipulator, prophet and sage.

In theory, the narrator of *Le Père Goriot* is indebted to Rastignac for information received (17). Balzac subscribes to this fiction—as long as it suits his purpose. He seems to rely on the young student to reconstruct Goriot's past and to introduce us into society; moreover it is rare that he gives us a direct view into the minds of the other characters. But there is much that occurs when Rastignac is not on stage, and even when he is, the author's vision goes beyond that of his informant (as, for example, in the scene of the quarrel in Chapter IV where gestures are described which the hidden Rastignac could not possibly have observed). Balzac alone is in possession of total knowledge; he alone can explain, justify and evaluate the total work. And he exploits his privilege to the full,

---

[1] Wayne C. Booth, *The Rhetoric of Fiction*, Chicago, 1961, p. 1.

generalizing on experience, commenting on the work, and making overt advances to his readers.

*

In *Le Père Goriot* there are well over a hundred generalizations, ranging in length from a single sentence to a whole paragraph. Not surprisingly it is in the early part of the novel that Balzac's voice is most in evidence: the first two chapters (which are only slightly longer than the last two) contain over 80 per cent of the general comments. The second chapter alone contains half the total number: Balzac, dealing with his young hero's entry into society, is here most obviously at pains to stress the universality of his subject. This chapter contains a fair cross-section of the moral, psychological and sociological generalizations employed throughout: there are observations on tailors (111), money (112), student life (112–13), projection of ideas (114), youth (134), physiognomy (135), temptation (136), gratitude (137), gastronomy (138), education (139), corruption (147), emotion (152), fashion (158), love-affairs (158), temperaments (158), boarding-houses (159), society (166), Paris (168), prodigality (173), and women (175–6 *et passim*!). The reader is obviously supposed to be impressed with this parade of information and erudition, most of which emerges from the narrative without undue strain. And Balzac varies his rhetoric to suit the occasion; the generalizations differ considerably in extent, structure and tone, though a few set patterns predominate.

Two of the most common phrases in this context are of the type 'un de ces (gens) qui . . .', and 'ces (jolis rêves) que (font tous les jeunes gens)'; between them these two patterns account for over a third of all the generalizations. In both instances the specific is subordinated to the general, and an implicit appeal is made to the reader's experience. The first phrase is often used to introduce a character, including such dissimilar persons as Rastignac, Poiret and Vautrin. The primary intention may be to emphasize typicality (Rastignac), to indicate nonentity (Poiret) or to strike a casual note (Vautrin—who first appears disguised as a popular and expansive member of the boarding-house). Rather than confer immediate individuality on these people, Balzac begins by placing them in a larger category, and he does so in an informal manner, reminiscent of the tone we adopt when we are about to indulge in gossip. The same syntactical pattern is used indiscriminately to describe houses (139, 160), furniture (148–9), glance (82, 87, etc.) and gesture (168, etc.); it is a mannerism which betrays an inordinate fondness for assigning a general significance to an incident or object of minor importance. There is also present (particularly with the second type of phrase) an air of self-assurance and a failure to be explicit which becomes irritating; such remarks as 'cette admirable puissance que possèdent les femmes' (73) or 'cette force de passion qui plaît tant aux femmes' (44) do little either to define the emotion in question or to convince us of the author's perspicacity.

This tendency to indulge in dogmatic assertion is frequent in Balzac, and takes many forms, ranging from apophthegms to rather heavy epigrams, from brief prefatory observations to lengthy expositions. A particular action may be prefixed by an uncompromising assertion ('comme toutes les femmes, elle . . .') or followed by a scaffolding of general remarks which are to provide both embellishment and support. The dogmatic remarks can be broken down into two main groups, the first containing conventional generalizations by means of which Balzac sets himself in a well-established tradition, the second including observations which are peculiarly his own. Most of the former the reader takes in his stride. They are familiar and reassuring; perhaps, to some, rather tedious:

Il est dans la nature des femmes de prouver l'impossible par le possible et de détruire les faits par des pressentiments (168).

L'amour est une religion, et son culte doit coûter plus cher que celui de toutes les autres religions (245) etc.

Some of the latter, especially the shorter comments, momentarily startle by a mixture of the commonplace and the unusual:

Les passions ne font jamais de faux calcul (152).

L'insuccès nous accuse toujours la puissance de nos prétentions (169).

Le sentiment s'empreint en toutes choses et traverse les espaces (135).

The last of these may appear, as a bald statement, absurd; and yet the reader has been prepared for it by the (admittedly fanciful) argument which precedes it, and by other remarks and actions in the novel. On page 114 Balzac, in the long paragraph beginning 'Sans doute les idées se projettent en raison directe de la force avec laquelle elles se conçoivent,' has given us a lecture on his theory of attraction, repulsion and contagion: ideas are forces which can be projected through space, and emotions exercise a spell on those within range. As scientific reasoning the paragraph has its drawbacks, but as a dramatized commentary on the clash between Vautrin and Rastignac, and as a metaphorical expression of the interplay of forces which constitute Balzac's universe, it is a passage which adds significantly to our understanding of the work.

We must be careful, then, to situate Balzac's generalizations, to examine them in context. It is rare that they are purely gratuitous observations, even though some have obviously been included to impress the public. Balzac, like Proust, believed in 'Laws' of behaviour, fixed patterns which dictate and explain our actions; he also clearly felt the need to justify his work and to explain the motives of his characters in other than arbitrary terms. It is true that at times his logic is suspect, as, for example, at the end of Chapter I when he is attempting to 'prove' the existence of Goriot's passion; having described the man's 'typical' stupidity and ignorance, Balzac moves on to establish the emotional context by means of a pair of breath-taking generalizations: 'Ces natures se ressemblent presque toutes. A presque toutes, vous trouveriez un sentiment sublime au cœur' (102–3). And on other occasions (notably on pages 41, 70 and 115), the particular example is deduced ('donc') from a speculative generalization which has obviously been erected on the basis of the particular example itself! Philosophers may find this objectionable; most readers of novels do not notice such things, and those who do, if they are under the spell, smile, as Proust did, and forgive.

Like Proust, Balzac builds many of his demonstrations on to the original framework of the novel; of the one hundred and twenty or so generalizations, thirty-five were not included in the original manuscript. The basic narrative develops into a general vision of humanity; the additions indicate an imagination which moves from the particular towards the universal. Balzac, re-reading his manuscript, senses the possibility of enlarging the significance of event, situation or psychological trait; and rather than relying on the reader to move beyond the confines of private and local circumstance, he leads him triumphantly towards the desired goal. Some of the additions are short statements which summarize, emphasize, explain:

> Les jeunes gens de province ignorent combien est douce la vie à trois (72).

> Sachez-le bien, une femme aimante est encore plus ingénieuse à se créer des doutes qu'elle n'est habile à varier le plaisir (80).

On a dozen occasions large blocks of material of a basically expository nature are grafted on to the original narrative; this is particularly true in scenes which concern Rastignac (e.g. pp. 40, 173, 244–6), and I believe we can see here more evidence of Balzac's desire to shift the focus of the novel on to his young hero. Other additions concern generalizations used by the characters themselves (see especially 124–6, 128 and 130 for

Vautrin); Balzac's people share his weakness for large pronouncements, and indeed it is often difficult to distinguish their voice from his own. Like Balzac, Vautrin draws grand moral conclusions from specific aspects of Parisian life; like Balzac, he is an autodidact, and proud of it; and his generalizations have the same dogmatic overtones, and contain the same mixture of the obvious, the striking and the extravagant as those of his creator.

*

Balzac not only exploits his characters as direct vehicles for his own view of the world, he also comments directly upon them as individuals and as participants in the drama. In the main his preferences are clear. We have already considered (in Chapters II and IV) the manner in which judgment is implicitly passed on some characters by means of description and imagery. And Balzac on occasion takes sides more frankly: Madame Vauquer, Poiret, Michonneau and the mass of the boarders are the recipients of his direct scorn; Madame de Beauséant is openly admired: 'cette femme était vraiment aussi bonne que grande' (138). Rastignac, Vautrin and Goriot are less unambiguously treated. On occasions Balzac is sharply critical of his young hero; he refers to him as 'l'imprudent' (71), 'enfant' (96), 'cet élégant inédit' (77), and draws attention to his clumsiness and inexperience. And yet Balzac is tolerant of many of Rastignac's faults and reserves for him a special tenderness and protectiveness, as if he saw in the apprentice dandy his own ambitions and temptations, and as if, perhaps, he envied his success. The long passages of analysis on pages 40–1 (where Rastignac is described as 'un jeune homme ardent et spirituel') and on page 114 are basically sympathetic; and Balzac throughout is at pains to demonstrate the sensitivity and spontaneity of his hero. But he does not shirk the task of censuring Rastignac for his ethical relativism; we are made aware of the distance that separates Rastignac from men of true rectitude (147), and Balzac can be sharply critical of his hero's moral cowardice (276). Affection and comprehension do not in this case preclude judgment.

Vautrin presents a more difficult problem. Direct comments usually serve only to increase the mystery of the man and to emphasize his diabolical power; he is 'démon' (178), 'tentateur' (179), 'terrible sphinx' (138). And in a short summarizing paragraph after Vautrin's capture, ethical concern is subordinated to esthetic appreciation: Balzac describes his villain as 'un poème infernal' (224), and causes one of the boarders to exclaim: 'il est fameusement beau à dessiner' (226). Fascination with Vautrin's limitless capacity for unrepentant evil seems to cause a paralysis of Balzac's moral sense, resulting in a suspension of sentence.

With regard to Goriot there is evidence of a subtle mixture of contempt (for his ignorance and blindness), criticism (for his perversion), admiration (for his heroism) and compassion (for his suffering). Part of Goriot's complexity undoubtedly springs from the multiformity of the author's judgments, which range from 'l'ouvrier stupide et grossier' (102) to 'ce Christ de le Paternité' (238). It is not surprising to find our own reactions far from clear cut, for our total view of a character is partly dependent on the opinions openly expressed by the narrator. With his three major characters Balzac seems to prefer an ambiguous response; our final assessment must be made from a perspective that is ultimately our own.

But Balzac is anxious that the significance and relevance of central themes in the novel be clearly understood. He early draws attention to the grief and suffering which lie beneath the turbulent surface of Parisian life, and points out the need for a compassionate reaction to Goriot's misfortunes. Later, speaking of Rastignac, he suggests the general lessons to be learned from the individual example, and manages at the same time to introduce some modest propaganda in his own behalf:

S'il était bien peint dans sa lutte avec Paris, le pauvre étudiant fournirait un des sujets les plus dramatiques de notre civilisation moderne (139–40).

Unlike Stendhal who tends to play down the importance of his material and often treats his work in a cavalier fashion, Balzac comments on the seriousness and veracity of his work, and deliberately intensifies its nature. It is a 'drame' (5), an 'obscure, mais effroyable tragédie parisienne' (105). In the latter quotation the words 'mais effroyable' were added in the *Revue de Paris* edition, and we find a similar addition on page 222, where the author comments on a particular aspect of his own creation, describing Vautrin's capture as an 'horrible et majestueux spectacle!' It is as if Balzac has become his own spectator and is unable to refrain from giving us his reactions. Few readers, I think, will resent these somewhat naïve authorial observations; even if we consider them an unwarranted pre-emption of our own responses, we recognize in them evidence of Balzac's involvement which increases our own sense of wonder. Indeed if we remain indifferent to the obvious delight which the author takes in his own creation, I do not see how we can persevere with Balzac for very long.

*

Balzac shows himself aware of the audience he hoped to obtain. Early in the novel he addresses a hypothetical reader who, seated in a comfortable chair, will pick up the book saying: 'Peut-être ceci va-t-il m'amuser.' Balzac continues:

> Après avoir lu les secrètes infortunes du père Goriot, vous dînerez avec appétit en mettant votre insensibilité sur le compte de l'auteur, en le taxant d'exagération, en l'accusant de poésie. Ah! sachez-le: ce drame n'est ni une fiction, ni un roman. *All is true*, il est si véritable, que chacun peut en reconnaître les éléments chez soi, dans son cœur peut-être (6–7).

Like Diderot before him, Balzac realizes that the words 'fiction' and 'roman' are associated in the minds of the reading public with exaggeration, fantasy, flight from reality. In attempting to demolish such preconceptions, he warns us against identifying ourselves with those frivolous, leisured consumers for whom art is mere entertainment. He urges a commitment to the search for truth and a participation which includes self-contemplation; we are to become the readers of ourselves as well as the companions of the narrator.

A modern audience, accustomed to more modest claims and subtler overtures, may resent being buttonholed in this peremptory manner; such overt rhetoric is usually associated with the humorous self-indulgence of a Fielding or a Sterne. Balzac's method of establishing a relationship with his readers is certainly uncompromising in this instance, though he does later make concessions and appeals. In the description of the boarding-house, for example, he brings the reader into the picture with the use of 'vous' (pp. 8, 11), and establishes complicity by inviting us to share his judgment: 'l'un de ces hommes dont *nous* disons . . .' (20). Moreover, on occasions unambiguous assertion yields to hypotheses and suppositions. In the portraits of Mademoiselle Michonneau and Poiret, for example, Balzac appears unsure of details concerning origins and motivation, and limits himself to a series of interrogatives: 'Quel acide avait dépouillé . . .', 'était-ce le vice, le chagrin, la cupidité?' (18), etc.; 'Quel travail avait pu le ratatiner ainsi?' (19), etc. For a moment, at least, the God-like author appears to become human, and the reader is flattered by the equality of status thus afforded.

Such instances are less uncommon in Balzac than is usually supposed. There are some twenty occasions in *Le Père Goriot* on which uncertainty is professed by means of such expressions as 'peut-être', 'sans doute', 'soit . . . soit', or by the verbs 'devoir' and 'sembler'. In most cases the hypotheses or alternatives do not bear on questions of major importance, and it would seem that Balzac is simply exploiting a traditional device to make a perfunctory gesture in the direction of the reader. It matters little, as far as the action of the novel is concerned, whether Poiret has worked in the Ministry of Justice or in a slaughter-house (19)! But more significant issues are occasionally left in doubt; a notable example occurs on pages 175–6, where Balzac is attempting to account for Delphine's ascendency over Rastignac. The long passage of analysis contains a series of guesses by which the author, perplexed, endeavours to establish motivation. The reader is forced to make his own assessment of the true situation, and thus he becomes more actively involved in the drama.

Two other methods of inviting collaboration are preterition, and what one may call the 'multiple appeal'. The first of these is sometimes exploited with humorous intent (as, for example, on page 11 where Balzac writes of the *odeur de pension*: 'Peut-être pourrait-elle se décrire si l'on inventait un procédé pour évaluer les quantités élémentaires et nauséabondes qu'y jettent les atmosphères catarrhales . . .' etc.); elsewhere references to other arts, notably to painting, are used to compel the reader to complete an image which the author appears unable to evoke in words (e.g. on page 238 during the description of Goriot as 'ce Christ de la Paternité'). This kind of oblique directing of the imagination is accompanied elsewhere by appeals to experience and judgment. Balzac at times flatteringly invites us to identify ourselves with 'un homme de bon sens' (139) or with 'les jeunes gens supérieurs' (40), in order to persuade us to share his vision. Deference is paid to our desire to know how authorial opinion is arrived at: 'Chacun comprendra mieux . . . après une remarque . . .' (183–4). It is presumed (pp. 5–6) that we are familiar with Parisian life and can therefore subscribe to the overall truth of the narrative and to the particular relevance of the epigram 'quand on connaît Paris, on ne croit à rien de ce qui s'y dit, et l'on ne dit rien de ce qui s'y fait' (168). Secure in the knowledge that many of his readers are women, Balzac does not neglect to call upon them to testify to the accuracy of his analysis: 'Et quelle femme ne l'aurait cru comme elle . . . ?' (193). Youthful readers (and those who still recall the illusions and disappointments of adolescence) are particularly invited to become involved in the travails of Rastignac. And, finally, we are all expected to share the author's indignation and compassion as he recounts the 'secrètes infortunes du père Goriot' (6). Whereas Stendhal rarely concedes anything to his reader and haughtily addresses his works to the 'happy few', Balzac (who had good reasons for refusing to limit his circulation) aims at a wide audience with whom he appears anxious to be on good terms.

And yet, in spite of attempts to solicit our participation and assent, Balzac remains essentially an autocratic creator, master of the material which so obviously fascinates him. If at times he expresses uncertainty, and appears on the defensive, he far more frequently reveals a thorough-going knowledge of character and situation. Indeed there are occasions on which he suggests that more information is available than he is willing to impart. This is obviously true for the 're-appearing characters', but even in the case of Victorine, of whom we learn that 'son histoire eût fourni le sujet d'un livre' (21), we are made to feel there is much being left unsaid. One senses, indeed, that Balzac, if he so wished, could develop the total existence of any of his characters, and make of it the central issue of a novel. As it is, we have to content ourselves with what he chooses to reveal.

*

Whether we like it or not, the author's voice in *Le Père Goriot* is a force to be reckoned with. Balzac propels his fiction resolutely forward and compels the reader to attend to its particular resonance and general meaning. He takes himself and his endeavour with high seriousness, conscientiously and robustly performing his many rôles. The words of Philarète Chasles, which Balzac probably dictated himself, are profoundly taken to heart:

> Le narrateur est tout. Il est historien; il a son théatre; sa dialectique profonde qui meut ses personnages; sa palette de peintre et sa loupe d'observateur (XI, 180).

Formerly, continues Chasles, it was the tale which was all-important; now the public is more demanding, asking for analysis and explanation as well as distraction: 'Soyez commentateur et *amuseur!*' Balzac, though he was certainly more interested in the gilding than the pill, gave his public its money's worth, partly no doubt because he hoped he was making a prudent investment, but also because, as he wrote in the *Avant-Propos*, he believed it was the writer's obligation to arrive at 'une décision quelconque sur les choses humaines' (I, 7).

The major decision arrived at, in *Le Père Goriot*, is neither original nor particularly profound; society is infamous, the noble heart is inevitably defeated, the world is a vale of tears. One by one the characters step forward and deliver their message and their warning, and the narrator joins his voice to theirs:

> [Rastignac] vit le monde comme il est: les lois et la morale impuissantes chez les riches, et vit dans la fortune l'*ultima ratio mundi* (95).

The central subject is unmistakably there and is brought home to us again and again through character, event and explicit judgment. But if the reader cannot miss it, he cannot but be profoundly moved and disturbed by it, such is the force generated by the total work.

Conclusion

In his famous article on *La Chartreuse de Parme* Balzac drew a distinction between literature of images (Hugo, Chateaubriand, Vigny) and literature of ideas (Voltaire, Mérimée, Stendhal), the former being lyrical and poetic, the latter characterized by sobriety, concision and irony. Unwilling to categorize himself as neatly as he catalogued others, Balzac created for himself (and a few privileged companions) a third school, that of literary eclecticism:

> Certaines gens complets, certaines intelligences *bifrons*, embrassent tout, veulent et le lyrisme et l'action, le drame et l'ode, en croyant que la perfection exige une vue totale des choses (CHH, XXVIII, 198).

The splendidly presumptuous statement reveals the grandiose scope of Balzac's endeavour; he strove for nothing less than an absolute view—of his times, of human experience and of the universe. The result is the elaborate structure of the *Comédie humaine* which, containing ninety-two works and three thousand characters, is of such formidable dimensions that it threatens to engulf the beholder. Even the admiring Henry James recognized the difficulty of achieving a focus, of doing justice to the whole. But it is the whole which ultimately must be tackled, for, as Victor Hugo was the first to realize, the *Comédie humaine* must stand or fall as a total achievement.

A reading of *Le Père Goriot* enables us to become acquainted with major characters and dominant themes, to begin an assessment of Balzac's creative process and to come to grips with his fictional techniques. Apparently simple, a Balzacian novel is in reality a complex and skilfully organized work of art. The structure of *Le Père Goriot*, like that of the *Comédie humaine*, is based on Balzac's deeply rooted tendency to express experience in antithetical terms. In *Le Père Goriot* two worlds are juxtaposed, the static unit of the boarding-house and the dynamic, disruptive confluence of Parisian society. Hostilities are uncovered between warring factions—daughters against father and against each other, criminal against society, idealistic youth against a cynical and corrupt civilization. And these basic patterns are complicated by moral and psychological conflicts within the characters themselves. Individuals who appear to represent a single attitude are in reality the theatre of opposing forces: noble passion versus perversion in Goriot, instinct versus control in Vautrin, idealism versus corruption in Rastignac, generosity versus egoism in Delphine. And Balzac's rhetoric, while apparently reducing experience to a series of unambiguous formulae, in fact increases the complexity and density of his world by establishing a network of conflicting comments and judgments which compel the reader to involve himself in the action of the novel and to form his own conclusions.

Throughout the *Comédie humaine* Balzac elaborates his vision of humanity by means of a similar dialectical process. His critics and biographers have called upon the myth of Prometheus to pay tribute to his genius, but it is significant that Balzac himself evokes the name of Janus when describing the activity of the artist. As one of his characters remarks:

Tout est bilatéral dans le domaine de la pensée. Les idées sont binaires. Janus est le mythe de la critique et le symbole du génie (IV, 789).

In spite of his attempt to rival the gods, Balzac was aware, as we have seen, of the limitations of man's powers; and this two-sided view of the human condition is reflected on every level of his thinking. He shared Rousseau's distrust of analysis and reasoning, portrayed the corrosive power of thought, and even considered genius a disease, possibly of demonic origin; on the other hand he believed that science would solve many of the mysteries which tormented him, and among his noblest characters are those who dedicate their lives to the pursuit of knowledge. His humanity, unified and organized on the pattern of the animal kingdom, reveals the predatory appetites of the jungle, and yet there are those who participate in an ascensional movement towards a higher state of being. In the realm of politics, Balzac admired stabilizing institutions even if they were reactionary and oppressive, and yet his vision of society was revolutionary, recognizing dynamic change. But although the self-assertive individual is admired for his defiance of the restrictions imposed by the collectivity, it is the group alone which can survive; for rampant individualism is seen as the greatest threat to enduring structures, particularly to the unit of the family—the 'véritable élément social' (I, 9).

Balzac sought to test out his conflicting theories by setting them in motion in a fictional world which is a self-contained experimental laboratory with windows opening out on to reality. Ideas are injected into characters, propelled through the *Comédie humaine* in a dozen different guises, modified according to personality and developing situation, and set up against a dozen different antagonists. Ambition, for example, implies the dandies (Rastignac, de Marsay, Lucien de Rubempré), the idealists (Bianchon, d'Arthez, Michel Chrestien) and such independent figures as Vautrin, Nucingen and Goriot. Goriot himself leads to Hulot, Claës and Frenhofer, the men of extravagant passion; they, in their turn, suggest, by opposition, the constricting conservatism of the misers—Gobseck, Grandet, Godain, Rigou. It is this constant process of parallelism, echo and contrast which results in the astonishing complexity of the *Comédie humaine*.

Fictional interrelationships are doubled by indirect links with contemporary figures: Rastignac resembles Thiers, Vautrin recalls Vidocq, d'Arthez is based on Buchez, Canalis could be Lamartine or Hugo. Balzac's world, though primarily an independent repertory with its own index and cross-references, is also a vast directory which provides a record of a critical period in French history. Concentrating primarily on the fortunes of a triumphant bourgeoisie, Balzac found himself facing the problem which was to confront his successors: if the novel is to be concerned with the recording of contemporary experience, how can it attain dignity and value in a society whose dominant class, obsessed with material possessions, is moving towards mediocrity and conformity? Balzac's response, as historian and as novelist, is to inject significance into the lives of ordinary persons who become the representatives not only of basic human tendencies but also of social and historical forces. Thus in *Le Père Goriot* Vautrin is both the personification of temptation and the incarnation of anarchy, 'le type de toute une nation dégénérée, d'un peuple sauvage et logique, brutal et souple' (224). Rastignac's career demonstrates the manner in which the impoverished nobility integrated itself into the new society, accepting alien values. Goriot takes us through Revolution and Empire and shows how, by skilful manipulation and a good sense of timing, a simple workman could earn a fortune and place his daughters in positions of social prominence. Balzac thus surveys and judges his society which he represents in terms of movement, assimilation and conflict; the old order has been destroyed and is being replaced by a society which lacks purpose and direction. The Goriot family, ruptured by greed and passion, and casting off the authority of the father, may be taken as a symbol of the country as a whole.

*

Le Père Goriot was written at a time when the novel in France was still seeking respectability and attempting to establish itself as a major genre worthy of serious critical consideration. In the *Avant-Propos* to the *Comédie humaine* (written in 1842), Balzac expressed his debt to Walter Scott whom he admired for having given 'une allure gigantesque à un genre de composition injustement appelé secondaire' (I, 6), and he undoubtedly considered, correctly, that he was undertaking a similar revolution in France. In *Le Père Goriot*, as we have seen, he felt it necessary to insist on the truth of his narrative and to disassociate himself from 'fictions' and 'novels', as if his readers would naturally be inclined to connect his work with extravagance, immorality and falsehood; and we have only to glance at the majority of novels published in the eighteen-twenties (including some of Balzac's own youthful potboilers) in order to applaud this high-minded declaration of principle.

But Balzac, as we immediately discover, did not possess the uncompromising aloofness of a Flaubert. He remained very much aware of the moods and desires of his immediate public, and he considered it part of his function to provide tears, thrills and laughter, as well as matter for reflection. Like Dickens, he was fascinated by the mysterious, the bizarre and the melodramatic, and he delighted in confronting his readers with grotesque figures and sudden irruptions of drama. Mobilizing all the forces of language and all the resources of his craft, he compelled his material to yield grandiose and dazzling effects with which he himself was clearly delighted. *Le Père Goriot* is both a revolutionary exposure of contemporary reality and a splendid tribute to Balzac's own exuberant nature.

Every reader has to come to terms with this exuberance, flamboyance and self-adulation. There are few people, I suspect, who have not, at one time or another, fallen under Balzac's spell; some of them, returning to reality, resent the power which usurped their freedom, and accuse the magician of cheap and vulgar sleight of hand. They express their indignation by drawing up lists of his grammatical errors, tawdry metaphors and lapses of taste, objecting to phrases like 'ce Christ de la Paternité' and to such characters as Trompe-la-Mort. Comparing Balzac's style to a hypothetical norm and his characters to people in the street, they accuse him of distortion, falsification and bombast. Such readers usually seek consolation in Stendhal. Others, less severe, retain their affection and continue to read Balzac as they read detective stories, compulsively and uncritically. They pay tribute to what is perhaps the novelist's greatest gift—his ability to tell a story—but they are unable to take Balzac seriously and unwilling to believe that a writer who is so superb an entertainer can be a great novelist.

It is certainly true that Balzac seems, even to those who admire him the most, curiously inaccessible, and as impenetrable as some of his own characters. Percy Lubbock puts it down to Balzac's 'obviousness' which initially blocks the critic's imagination. But a re-reading of the novels leads to a re-evaluation: '[His greatness] has . . . depths and recesses that did not appear till now. . . . One after another, the rarer, obscurer effects of fiction are all found in Balzac, behind his blatant front.'[1] Lubbock's

[1] Percy Lubbock, *The Craft of Fiction*, New York, 1957, p. 204.

view is echoed by the contemporary French novelist, Michel Butor, who expresses his admiration in similar terms: 'Il est peu de lecture . . . qui soit plus enrichissante aujourd'hui pour un romancier, qui introduise mieux le lecteur aux problèmes du roman contemporain.'[1] This latter testimony from one of the 'nouveaux romanciers' may at first appear unexpected, for it often seems (from the theoretical writings of Robbe-Grillet and Nathalie Sarraute, for example) that the Balzacian novel is considered an outmoded form by modern writers who have moved away from 'typical' characters and 'artificial' plots in search of a purer, less blatantly manipulated fiction.

Irreverent readers will perhaps maintain that an injection of Balzac into the flat, dehumanized surfaces of the modern French novel would be of considerable therapeutic value. At all events, I find it an invigorating experience to turn back to a novelist who admits to an urgent commitment to his own characters and who brings to the contemplation of everyday existence a purposeful curiosity and a sense of wonder. Balzac's energetic response to the life he observes and the forms he creates continues to strike a compelling and original note. In *Le Père Goriot* he demonstrates his ability to establish a firm and idiosyncratic hold on reality, to forge connections between individual characters and universal forces, and to discover a form appropriate to his passion for drama. The novel's strength lies not in the passive mirroring of things as they are, but in intensification and amplification; and Balzac convinces us of the value of imaginative distortion. Involving us in a process of elaboration, demolition and reconstruction, he compels us to come to terms with his vision of life and to reflect upon the limitless possibilities of fiction.

[1] Michel Butor, *Répertoire*, Paris, 1960, p. 93.